# MENTAL HEALTH / MENTAL ILLNESS

McGraw-Hill
Series in
Health Education

Deobold B. Van Dalen, *Consulting Editor*

# MENTAL HEALTH /
# MENTAL ILLNESS:
## Revolution in Progress

**LEALON E. MARTIN**

*Associate Director*
*Office of Communications*
*National Institute of Mental Health*

**McGraw-Hill Book Company**
New York   St. Louis   San Francisco   Düsseldorf   London
Mexico   Panama   Sydney   Toronto

*616.89*
*M36*
*c.*

This book was set in Electra by Rocappi, Inc.,
and printed on permanent paper and bound by Vail-Ballou Press, Inc.
The designer was Barbara Ellwood.
Sally Ellyson supervised the production.

# MENTAL HEALTH /
# MENTAL ILLNESS

*Library of Congress Catalog Card Number 77-118867*

07-040644-8
07-040643-X

234567890   VBVB   7987654321

To Lucile, Cile, and Lynne,
whose love *is* mental health

Conscious life begins, continues, and ends through the mind—man's brain and nervous system. Knowledge of the health and illnesses of the mind, therefore, is of interest and importance to everyone. The book is for students, teachers, or general readers who want a reasonably comprehensive amount of information on mental illness/mental health for personal or professional use.

A vast body of information concerning mental health and mental illness has accumulated through the ages. Obviously, no one book nor even several volumes could include all this information. Although this book is selective, it includes a wide range of information which serves as a foundation for learning about mental illness and mental health.

The farther back in time we go, the easier it is to spot bits of information and theories which have withstood the erosions of scientific, political, or popular questioning. The closer to the present we come, however, the more difficult it is to separate loose claims, or even good hypotheses, from solidly based work—and poor programs from sound programs. Nonetheless, this book bravely tells the reader more about what we *think* we know today than about what we are *sure* we know of the past. More bravely still, a nod, a look, a sidelong glance is given to tomorrow.

This book is in a sense a "cause" publication. It postulates first-rank importance for mental illness and mental health. This book does not propose to present any one speciality's position nor to support any one school of thought, but rather to examine divergent as well as concurrent viewpoints. Associations relevant to the mental health field will also be covered.

There are a great many books on particular aspects of mental illness/mental health, which have been written by psychiatrists, psychologists, social workers, nurses, administrators, medical historians, professional writers, mentally ill people, theorists with a cause to sell, and "healers." Specialization is often apparent in the titles. There are fewer overall approaches, general books, or syllabi. It is hoped that this book will help fill a need for such a general approach.

Mental illness, it has been said, is everybody's business. Mental health, it might be said, is not only everybody's business, but also the individual's most important business: because it is solely up to him to obtain and to give as much "mental health" as possible if he wants a happy life. Each day, every man encounters mental or emotional problems of his own—and of his fellow man. Each day, many times a day, he attempts to overcome or prevent some mental trouble and to influence the mental processes of his fellow man.

Each of these actions and thoughts involves an act of communication. Every act of communication is itself, in a sense, an action for or against mental illness or mental health.

If communication is more effective and thoughtfully used, mental health will be improved and mental illness reduced—for you, the individual, and for your fellows. If this book increases the reader's knowledge about mental illness/mental health and offers him useful and interesting information, it will have well served its objective.

The objective, in a word, is to summarize the relevant facts about mental illness/mental health—a revolution in progress.

LEALON E. MARTIN

# CONTENTS

# HISTORICAL HIGHLIGHTS

## CHAPTER ONE

Mental illness is as old as man. Undeveloped as they were mentally, progenitors of Homo sapiens had mental troubles, as did Homo sapiens himself. The pre-people and their descendants worried about predators; they suffered accidents and fevers that damaged their minds; and they inflicted injury to the minds of others in fights. Ever since, man has been trying desperately to explain mental illness, to cope with it, and to find mental health. His first explanations were simple. He attributed mental disorders to natural phenomena, the malevolent influence of other men, or evil spirits.

Any one of the forerunners of sapient man must have occasionally had concern for mental health. He may have had to comfort a

mate who was behaving wildly. He may have shouted defiantly at
the dark skies in order to clear his mind when awaking from a
nightmare in which he was slashed by a tiger's claws. Man, it is
obvious today, still finds mental ill health—and the matter of removing the *ill* from before the *health*—the most stubborn puzzle
of the ages.

Some of our dealings with the "coin" of mental matters, with
illness on the one side and health on the other, are as old as
prehistory and as new as tomorrow. Endlessly the game goes on:
the coin is flipped in the hope that it will turn up on the mental
health side. Today, it appears that the chances are still about 50:50
for either side of the coin to show. But tomorrow may offer another story, for science may be catching up at last with matters of
the mind—the toughest of all fields to research. Before tomorrow,
and while today lasts, look for a moment at man's past concern
with his mind and its troubles. Retrospect gives perspective and a
framework for understanding the current scene and the future's
prospects.

## BEFORE RECORDED HISTORY

Early man often had mental troubles as well as such physical ailments as infections, arthritis, respiratory and intestinal diseases, and
arteriosclerosis. He did not endure his mental disorders as long as
we do, for his short life-span would not allow it. But early man did
seek to cope with mental illness. He regarded it and treated it,
most likely, in the same way as he did his physical illnesses. To him
an infected tooth was caused by the same things that made another
individual a raving person: evil spirits or lightning or enemies'
spells. Thus, for both mental illness and physical illness, he used
such "treatments" as rubbing, licking, sucking, cutting, and binding;
or salves, incantations, potions, and charms; or reverence, bribery,

and threats—or anything else his friends, his leaders, and he himself might think of.

But it is encouraging to know that, before the dawn of recorded history, man treated the mentally ill humanely. He did not cast the mentally disturbed from his society, seal them off in caves, or ridicule, beat, or kill them. Ignorant and savage though they were, our progenitors nonetheless dealt with mental illness in a fashion that was not to be seen on earth again to any great degree until very recent times.

All through recorded history, with few exceptions, civilizations have been characterized by maltreatment of the mentally ill, who were treated viciously and viewed as vermin. Moreover, contemporary man probably deals no more mercifully with mental disorders than did men of earlier ages.

What was mental illness like in early man? Was it different from mental illness today? There is no way of knowing for sure. It is a reasonable speculation that some of the manifestations of mental illness today are much like those of the ancient past. They may be "related," as we ourselves are related to the ancestors of our forefathers. Genetic theories of disease would at least not discourage such a view.

The causes of dawn-age mental illness may also be assumed to be related to the causes of mental illness in our time. Both internal factors (worry, say, over great numbers of predators in the neighborhood) and environmental factors (cruel weather, disappearance of food animals, failure of berries to show up one spring) played a part in the mental illness of early man.

Forerunners of our psychiatrists and psychologists began to appear in the earliest of times. As always in society, when a need arises, someone seeks to fill it. Thus the witch doctor came to the forefront. Mental illness, naturally, was a part of his practice. These witch doctors were often the better intellects of the group; perhaps some of them had kind inclinations toward others and found satisfaction in serving their fellows. Although the mentally and physically ill were treated without differentiation and compassionately on the whole, the witch doctors and group leaders did remove them if they or their sickness appeared to be hurting the group. Also, the sick were killed or left to die if there was no way to help or cure them.

As societies became more complex, bringing greater division of labor and opportunities for specialization, the art and business (it was hardly a science as yet) of helping others to heal grew in importance.

In every community, some of the witch doctors turned toward other, widening horizons as time marched on and religion became a major social institution. Thus, in many instances, the forerunner of the modern doctor was involved in the beginnings of organized religion. Early civilizations bear this out. Physicians were often priests. Looked upon as priests first and doctors second, they were nevertheless the community's physicians.

The association of medicine with religion persists quite substantially, of course, through our times. Many religious organizations are noted for their medical services, not only in missionary work abroad but also within their own countries. The ties of religion and mental illness, furthermore, are closer than those between religion and any other illness. There is, for example, the Academy of Religion and Mental Health, a well-known and active organization in the United States. There are few, if any, such formal arrangements to serve other major fields of disease, such as cancer and diseases of the heart and blood vessels. This is not strange. It is alleged that religion contributes greatly to mental health—and vice versa. And so usually it is, but not always.

### EARLY CIVILIZATIONS

In all the early civilizations we know of—in Mesopotamia, Egypt, the Hebraic lands, India, China, and the Americas—priests and magicians treated the mentally ill. Among all these civilizations, through the whole of ancient times (from 5000 B.C. to around A.D. 500), mental illness was fairly common. Along with other afflictions, but perhaps even more than most, disturbances of the mind became a constant fellow traveler to man as he moved toward an organized life. Medicine became more organized as civilizations became more sophisticated.

In Mesopotamia's Babylon and Nineveh, the first men of medicine were priests. This pattern has continued for thousands of years and exists even today. Mental illness was associated with demons, and its cure or treatment with exorcising by religious means and magic rituals.

The Babylonians were the first to study a patient's life history, to codify the physician's responsibility to his patient, and to advance social medicine. The cuneiform tables upon which they inscribed their codifications of law and customs represent the most striking, and perhaps the first, devotion to systems analysis and development seen in the world; and medicine and mental illness were given their full share of this orderliness.

In Egypt, as in other early civilizations, medicine was closely tied to religion. Although magical and linked to religion, with gods established for health protection, Egyptian medicine was advanced and rational in some respects. In Egyptian writings, the brain is described for the first time, and its involvement in mental processes is recognized. The Egyptians had a forerunner of our medical schools in the temple of Imhotep, the principal god of healing. At this temple medical school, which also contained a hospital, recreational and occupational therapy were developed for patients, and a kind of psychotherapy was practiced which resembles some of the most modern approaches to treatment of mental illness.

Priest-doctors, the belief in demons, and an approach to the treatment of mental illness which was similar to that of the Egyptians and Mesopotamians also characterized Hebrew medicine. But the belief in one God as the source of all life, including health and disease, was a principal difference between it and the medicine of other early civilizations. Many descriptions of what undoubtedly were kinds of mental illnesses are found in the Old and New Testaments. But the Hebraic concern was not only with religious involvement in these manifestations of mental disorders. It demonstrated as well a deep and continuing interest in the humanitarian aspects of medicine and social welfare. As Early as A.D. 490, there was a hospital in Jerusalem established solely for the mentally ill.

In Persian lands, demons were blamed for mental illnesses and all other diseases. Persian priest-physicians held that there were 99,999 diseases afflicting man—all of them caused by demons. There were various kinds of doctors to deal with them, such as "knife doctor," "herb doctor," and "word doctor." Struggles went on incessantly in every man, they believed. The body or physical forces sought pleasure; this was evil. The good mind or psychic forces or soul sought purity, virtue, and charity. The only way to win was to carry on a never-ending exorcism of the bad. Thus, all the emphasis in their medicine was on magic and religious procedures.

In the Far East, Hindu and Chinese medical methods were like those in Persia; there were similar beliefs in good and evil warring forces, bad demons invading the human body, and the inevitable exorcisms. The Chinese had their good spirit (Yang), who was opposed by the bad spirit (Yin). The Hindus had somewhat the same thing in the good Vishnu who fought the forces of the maleficent Siva. Perhaps the chief interest that early medicine in the Far East has for the study of mental health is found in some practices of Buddhism. The Buddhist emphasis on turning to one's inner self and withdrawing from the external world has overtones of psycho-therapy much like certain forms used today.

The early Far East civilizations—those to the west, around the Mediterranean, and also those in the Americas during the time of the Incas and Aztecs—had several common characteristics with regard to mental illness and health. In all these societies there was apparently a considerable amount of mental and emotional disorder. It was recognized and dealt with by religious medical men in the context of religion. Treatment included not only incantations, religious rites, magic, and rituals, but also drugs and even recreation and occupational therapies and diversions.

Until recent modern history, the greatest contributions to man's health, physical and mental, came from the Greeks. Unbroken traditions in medicine extend, in a continuity rare in man's concerns, from such great Greek physicians as Aesculapius and Hippocrates. In Greece, medicine began to break away from the domination of religion. The temples of health built for Aesculapius were shrines at first, but later became "hospitals." Mental patients were taken to the temples, where treatment was based on eliminating the cause of the disorders. It was long believed that mental illness was caused by either demonic or divine spirits. Incantations as well as pharmaceuticals, herb compounds, and juices were used to treat patients. Still, though the shrines were not built or run for medical purposes, it did happen that medical approaches arose unhindered by religious dogma.

Outstanding, both in his own time and through the ages, was Hippocrates. In a sense, he originated the methods still used by modern medicine. He observed, collected, and compared information about diseases and patients, recorded the observations carefully, and cautiously drew conclusions. Thus, from Hippocrates and other Greeks came such valuable contributions as the knowledge that natural phenomena cause diseases, that mental illness ought to be treated humanely and studied well, that certain diseases can be cured by using specific remedies, and that the brain is the center of intellectual activity. In essence, the major legacy to us from the Greeks in medicine—as well as in other areas of life—was the replacement of utter belief in supernaturalism with the belief that a rational explanation existed for human and environmental phenomena.

When Rome rose to dominance, Romans copied from the Greeks in medicine as they did in many other fields. A good deal of the medical knowledge in Rome came from Greek practitioners who were there seeking fame and fortune. One such practitioner was Asclepiades. Although he had received a medical education in Greece, he at first taught rhetoric in Rome instead of practising medicine. The story goes that after he revived an alleged corpse, he was permitted to participate in Roman medical society. Asclepiades' work was distinguished by a humane approach both to mental patients and to physically sick people. He believed in comfortable, attractive measures of treatment. This did nothing to harm his popularity in Rome.

Strangely enough, nonmedical thinking produced a uniquely Roman contribution to mental medicine. Cicero, a philosopher not likely to be thought of in connection with medicine or disease, made the bequest. He said that emotions could cause physical sickness. He observed that physical illnesses did have basic differences from mental illnesses.

A broad span of man's life on earth has been fleetingly surveyed— from several million years before Christ, through the classical era of Greece and Rome, and arbitrarily set as ending around A.D. 500. Summing up these years leaves the observer encouraged. Viewing the years that followed the fall of Rome brings despair.

The 1,000 years known as the Middle Ages brought an abrupt end to the short-lived early age of reason. Justifiably, this period has been known as the Dark Ages.

## DARK, DISTURBED AGES

Bestial cruelty, abysmal fear, and rampant superstition ruled too many men for what seem unending centuries when one reads about the relentless acts of ignorance recorded during the Dark Ages. Many good practices which had been established in medicine were discontinued, and worse than this, the fearful superstition of pre-Greek times again became the chief characteristic of medicine.

The mentally ill were called witches in the thirteenth century, and torture and persecution became their treatment. They were blamed for many of society's difficulties as the common man and the authorities searched for scapegoats. Devastating fires or epidemics could easily be laid to the door of a man, woman or child who was considered to manifest aberrant behavior and who was therefore thought to be a witch. The witch-hunts of the thirteenth and fourteenth centuries were awesome displays of mob violence marked by mass psychoses.

Thus, the hunt was on; and none could have known then that just around a corner of time's corridor lay the printing press and gunpowder. One would open men's minds to the light of intelligence, and the other would blow out their brains; both would put a sharp end to the Dark Ages.

But all was not dark in the world during this period. In the Arabian countries, medicine and science grew along with the birth and growth of Islamic religion. Although mathematics was the greatest contribution of the Arabs—they gave us algebra and the concept of zero—they also made medical developments of note. Concerned with all sicknesses, the Arabs built hospitals early in the development of their civilization. There were many hospitals in their cities, and the mentally ill were treated either in them or in special hospitals established for mental disorders alone. Among the first of these was a mental hospital built in Fez, Morocco, in the early 700s. Another unusual mental hospital is reported as having been estab-

lished in Damascus during the twelfth century. It was free—all
mentally ill persons were treated without charge.


## THE RENAISSANCE

With the coming of the Renaissance, amid the rant of superstition
and religious frenzy, the clear call of enlightenment began to be
heard. Such a call could come only from an able and fearless man
who could cut through the shrouds of ignorance and reach enough
people with lucid reason to establish beachheads of knowledge.
Such a man was Johann Weyer.

Born in 1515 at Grave, Holland, on the Meuse River, Weyer went
to Paris for his doctorate in medicine, which he received in 1537.
During half a century of medical practice, he became a celebrated
physician. His consuming interest, in spite of skills in several fields
of physical medicine, was in mental disorders. He pointed out that
the so-called witches were merely mentally sick, or they were feign-
ing their alleged magical and evil knowledge. Weyer thus launched
a campaign which he carried on in spite of caustic criticism from
many supporters of witch-hunting—Martin Luther, the Pope, and
Dr. William Harvey, the great discoverer of how the heart and
circulatory system function.

During the sixteenth century, a million persons are said to have
been burned for witchcraft. The toll, great as it is, might have been
larger but for Weyer. His crusade was a small but potent beginning
to enlighten men and to help the mentally ill, who included most
of the witches. During his medical practice, he concentrated for
over thirty years on studying, while treating, the mentally ill. In his
work, he brought psychiatric treatment, which he provided for his
patients, into medicine. This marked the beginning of psychiatry as
a new medical specialty.

Though there was some progress in the sixteenth and seventeenth

centuries, much greater achievements were to come in the next
century.

## AN "AGE OF REASON"

Early in the eighteenth century, which sought to be an "Age of
Reason," there was great concentration upon classifications and
systems—a manifestation which might be found comparable to the
current concern with systems analysis.

Advances in physical medicine were achieved in identifying, studying, and trying to rationally treat many diseases hitherto left to
mystery and magic: diphtheria, neuralgia, typhus, typhoid, meningitis, angina pectoris (heart pain), chicken pox, smallpox, and others.
Edward Jenner proved that inoculation with cowpox could prevent
smallpox; Withering found an old wives' treatment—a compound
(digitalis) from the foxglove plant—helpful for heart patients; and
great progress was made in surgery.

Mental health profited not only from the stirrings in medical fields,
but also from social and political movements. This was the age of
revolution as well as reason, the age of Voltaire, Diderot, and
Rousseau, and the age of Thomas Paine, Benjamin Franklin, and
Thomas Jefferson. In England, Italy, and France crusades were
mounted against the chaining and prisoning of mental patients.
Chiaruggi led the crusade in Italy, Daniel Tuke in England, and
Philippe Pinel in France.

Pinel moved upon perhaps the most dramatic stage to achieve both
liberation from chains and humane study and treatment of the
poor unfortunates who were known universally in those days as the
mad or the insane. It was in the midst of, in spite of, or perhaps
even because of, the French Revolution that he, a gentle physician,
carried on his famed work. While revolution raged, Pinel went into
two prisons in France, at Bicêtre and Salpétrière. Through the

permissive support of revolutionary leaders who were not unhappy
at the overthrow of any part of the establishment, Pinel ordered
the shackles and chains removed from the mentally ill. He culmi-
nated his lifetime of devotion to mental health by observing and
classifying mental diseases in enormous detail.

### PSYCHIATRY: A NEW SPECIALTY

Following the 1700s, there were efforts to help the mentally ill in
the 1800s; but by the end of the century, physicians had not found
the causes of, nor prevention, cure, or effective treatments for,
mental illness—though they had classified thousands of kinds of
disorders.

The wide-ranging progress of other medical fields was opening
men's minds to more and more possibilities, among which could be
included the concept that mental health/mental illness were subject to scientific, medical, and community attack. Thus, in the
1800s, psychiatry came into recognition as a medical specialty. It
was associated with neurology (the study of the brain and the
nervous system) and still is to an extent, though the partnership has
not always been an easy one. Some diseases, such as syphilis and
blood-vessel diseases that harden the brain's arteries, can cause
tissue damage in the brain and produce strange behavior and other
symptoms associated with mental illness.

During the nineteenth century, developments in mental health fell
into four general areas: more humane and rational treatment of the
mentally ill by society, moves to improve mental institutions and
their practices, the influential attention of great writers and philos-
ophers to psychology and human behavior, and a comprehensive
classification system for mental disorders that extends its effects
into our times.

In America, where witches were burned as in Europe, the first
revolution for humane treatment and improvement of institutions

began through the unfaltering determination of one woman—Dorothea Dix, a Massachusetts schoolteacher. Visiting a jail, the House of Correction in East Cambridge, in 1841, she saw how the mentally ill were maltreated. She went into asylums and was even more horrified at the shameful handling and foul living conditions. Miss Dix devoted the rest of her life, until she died in 1887, to improving mental institutions and the attitudes and practices of individuals and organizations toward the mentally ill. She succeeded in accomplishing much in her home state and in a number of other states; and over twenty new hospitals for the "insane" are reported to have been established because of her work. She also carried her crusade abroad and "awakened the conscience of the entire world."

Although psychiatry had become a part of medicine as a recognized specialty, it lacked coherence as a discipline. The scope of mental illness facing psychiatry was so broad that it was hard to know where the problem began and where it ended. This uncertainty was one of the legacies from the nineteenth century, but Sigmund Freud seemed competent enough to handle the mass of information and end the stagnation.

## THEN CAME FREUD

The study of mental illness in the twentieth century invariably brings to mind the name of Freud, who started as a neurophysiologist occupied with organic tangibilities but who later moved into another world. Born in 1856, Freud died in 1939, leaving the first half of the century indelibly stamped with his dramatic hallmark— psychoanalysis and the importance of the unconscious.

He turned from physiological studies to psychological explorations and developed his own theoretical systems. Encouraging patients to express freely anything that came to mind, he found that his technique of "free association" allowed both himself and his patients to understand that the bases of mental problems were in early life experiences. Sexual repression, he held, was a central theme in the development of psychological makeup. Thus, Freud came to create the psychological method of exploration which he called psychoanalysis.

Through psychoanalysis, Freud could gather and study information about a patient's dreams and interpret the possible meanings. He could collect and analyze information about a patient's mistakes, lapses of memory, and slips of the tongue. Hidden conflicts of inner, perhaps unrecognized, motives could be examined.

Freud also believed that we are unconscious of many mental processes because they occur outside our awareness. His concept of the "unconscious" explains many otherwise unaccountable emotions, desires, and impulses. Along with psychoanalysis, this concept is among his major contributions.

However, after its initial derisive and hostile rejection, it was psychoanalysis that produced hope that major victories might be made over mental illness or even, perhaps, that it might be conquered. Yet, psychoanalysis could not prove to be all that was hoped for. It made little headway as a therapy for manic depression and schizophrenia, which together constitute the vast bulk of mental disorders. Yet it was useful in treating neuroses such as hysteria.

Psychoanalysis also laid new bases for scientific studies which would not have been possible without its methodology. The challenging vistas Freud opened up attracted many brilliant minds and led to new schools of thought, such as those of Alfred Adler, Carl Jung, and, in America, Adolph Meyer.

Meyer especially exemplifies the progress in psychiatry that came about in the United States. Because much of it occurred through his efforts, he has been called the Dean of American Psychiatry. At forty-three, Meyer directed the first psychiatric clinic that was to function as a part of a university, medical school, and hospital. This was the Henry Phipps Psychiatric Clinic of The Johns Hopkins University in Baltimore. Meyer's work and teaching helped to advance the recognition of psychiatry by medicine. More important, perhaps, was his urging that the preservation of mental health should be sought along with the cure of mental illness.

Neither Meyer nor Freud received a Nobel prize for his work, and it was not until 1949 that a Nobel prize was awarded for work relating to mental illness. Walter F. Hess, a Swiss researcher, won the prize in the physiology and medicine category for discovering how organs of the body are controlled by specific parts of the brain.

Corecipient with him that year was Antonio E. Maniz, a Portuguese, who received the prize for his operation known as *prefrontal lobotomy*—surgical cutting of nerve fibers between the brain's front lobes and the rest of the brain. Having become popular in the 1940s, it was performed on thousands of "incurables." The operation is now out of favor and little used. Although it reduced violent conflicts in some patients, it left many either with no improvement or in a state of complacent vegetation for the rest of their lives.

These awards at midcentury showed that the scientific medical world recognized the treatment of mental illness for its advances, for its importance, and for its ability to be scientifically explored by modern research techniques.

Many gains in the natural and life sciences also aided in opening new fields for mental illness studies. Among them were such developments as biomedical engineering. Today's instruments, for example, allow a researcher studying sleep and dreams to monitor sleeping human volunteers and gather exact evidence of a kind and quantity never before possible.

# WHAT IS
# MENTAL ILLNESS?

## CHAPTER TWO

Man's brain is a large mass of nerve tissue encased in a bony skull for protection. Nerve cells of gray matter and nerve fibers of white matter make up the nerve tissue, which weighs less than a pound in an infant but which increases to around three pounds in an adult. The brain and spinal cord form the central nervous system, which is linked through nerve channels to every inch of the body to constitute the nervous system. This nervous system coordinates the intricate networks of mental and physical functions whereby the organism man lives.

This brief description suggests that the brain and body are indissolubly linked. Indeed they are—more intricately perhaps than any other link between organs and the rest of the body. The brain is a group of organs analogous to a committee whose members serve the whole human being. This multiplicity presents an almost illimitable host of difficulties that have to be overcome in order to find out all we need to know about the nature of mental illness. It is not that we lack a substantial body of information (as well as opinion and raw speculation) about mental illness and the brain, mind, and body. Within this body of literature, particularly in that of the mental health field, the word *mind* is used more often than *brain* as the inclusive term for man's total conscious states. *Brain* is used in this chapter, however, to mean *mind* as well—meaning *mind* in the sense of both a person's capacity for mental activity and the sum of his conscious states.

## MENTAL ILLNESS IS A VAST COMPLEX

What is mental illness? The research to develop definitive answers may never end, but useful classifications and definitions are available. In simplest terms, mental illness is a disorder, disease, or disturbance that keeps a person from living as happily and healthily as he—and perhaps others—would like. Considered more technically, it is a complex of brain disorders. The number that are identifiable is almost endless, and thousands of mental troubles have been enumerated. They range from emotional difficulties, sometimes brief although harmful, to chronic major disturbances. This range includes (1) conditions fully or partly caused by physiological disorders, (2) conditions attributable to psychic or unknown causes, and (3) conditions caused by a combination of psychic and physiological factors.

Definitions and classifications of mental illness have had a somewhat confusing history. Systematic attempts have been and are being made by many schools. None has achieved a really unifying, comprehensive approach to relevant fields such as medicine, psychiatry, psychology, and sociology. The situation is far from mystifying. Many other areas, particularly the "soft" life sciences as opposed to the "hard" physical sciences, suffer also from the lack of precise nomenclature and uniform classification. Within the life sciences, mental illness presents the most formidable array of difficulties to the classifier. Although other disease areas—cancer or cardiovascular diseases, for example—pose severe obstacles to classification, they at least are concerned with organic (and therefore more tangible) matters. These are more amenable to delineation than mental illness is.

Nonetheless, classifications and descriptions of mental illness have been achieved which are useful and which constitute a far from meager resource. At times this resource may seem to contain an overabundance of terminological riches; and those who seek to diagnose a case of mental illness are confronted with too many choices. This is true even for the highly trained. Professionals learn to live with these tools and to use them properly. But it is also possible for nonprofessionals to obtain a reasonably fair picture of mental illness, for purposes other than dealing with patients, without the fear of having obtained that sometimes dangerous thing, a little knowledge.

## CAUSES AND CLASSIFICATION

Organic and functional mental illnesses are classified according to their known or suspected causes. Organic mental illnesses are (1) those resulting from acquired injuries or diseases that have damaged the brain and (2) those resulting from congenital defects— inborn damage that affects the brain. Functional mental illnesses are those resulting from one or many causes, but which always involve psychic factors. Its major categories are the psychoses, neuroses, personality disorders and psychosomatic illnesses.

Such conditions as alcoholism, narcotic addiction, drug abuse, criminality, sexual deviations, suicidal behavior, and delinquency are not usually considered separate kinds of mental illnesses, but rather as personality disorders. However, the qualification *usually* does not mean *always* or *inevitably.* Alcoholism, for instance, is sometimes handled as an entity in itself. In addition, the signs and symptoms of the various kinds of mental illnesses frequently over-lap or duplicate each other, and many of the symptoms that will be cited later as illustrative of one kind of mental illness may be considered by authorities as also symptomatic of another grouping.

The groupings that follow summarize the major kinds of mental illness: psychoses, neuroses, personality disorders, psychosomatic ill-nesses, and organic brain disorders. Again, it must be emphasized that these groupings are not sharply exclusive of each other. Con-sidering individual case histories (which is not the province of this book), one would find that many persons present evidence which can be assigned to one or several classifications of mental illness. Or a person may show signs of more than one mental illness, just as he may simultaneously have more than one organic illness.

## PSYCHOSES: A MALEVOLENT BRANCH

The psychoses are the most violent branch of mental illness. They differ widely in symptoms, extent, and duration, from bad but periodical or disappearing to shattering and lifelong. Those suffer-ing from psychoses fill the mental hospitals. Time and again, statis-tics underline the fact that the majority of patients in state, federal, or private mental hospitals are suffering from some psychosis.

*Insanity*, a term in ever-diminishing use in the mental health field and even in popular usage, was formerly used to mean *psychosis*. Medically, a psychosis can be termed a severe form of mental disease in which the individual's personality function is extensively disorganized. The person generally experiences feelings alien to him, shows aberrant behavior, and suffers from distortions of real-ity. Usually, he loses most of his contact with real life; and all areas of his life are critically disturbed. Psychosis may be triggered by organic, toxic, or psychological factors, and it may begin with mi-nor behavior deviations unobserved by others and identifiable only by a professional. But, as personality disorganization progresses, behavior may become so aberrant that the illness is apparent to everyone. Strong inner conflicts break down the ego, and the individual becomes incapable of social living. He may have to be hospitalized. The chief kinds of psychoses are schizophrenia, and depression.

## Schizophrenia

Manifested through a galaxy of symptoms, schizophrenia is the most devastating of the major mental illnesses. More than one-half of the mental-hospital beds in the United States are occupied by people suffering from some form of schizophrenia. Sadly enough, most of these sufferers are in their most productive years: they are between the ages of fifteen and forty-five.

The term *schizophrenia* meaning "split personality," was applied early in the twentieth century (1911) to a group of mental conditions previously known as *dementia praecox*. Attacking most frequently the young and the middle-aged, schizophrenia is a chronic (long duration) psychosis. There is such a great variety of associated groups of conditions under the heading of schizophrenia that no set of symptoms is sufficient to describe all schizophrenic patients. As a matter of fact, progress against schizophrenia has been hampered by the inability to diagnose and distinguish persons afflicted by the disease.

Schizophrenia continues to resist adequate, comprehensive classification despite several decades of scientific effort. However, these efforts have resulted in a useful symptomology. Among the more common symptoms of schizophrenia usually described are:

1　Disregard of personal appearance.
2　Marked fluctuations in behavior: from sitting motionless to constantly rushing around.

3   Wide range of talk: from muteness to verbal streams of meaning-less jargon, which may suddenly stop.

4   Delusions and hallucinations: considered the most important signs. Such delusions may occur as a result of believing that one is the victim of a group plot; or hallucinations may be experienced, such as hearing voices, seeing visions, or smelling strange odors.

At the onset of schizophrenia, a person usually knows that significant emotional changes are taking place. He may then seek help, but in most cases either he does not, or just as tragically, he fails to find suitable help. As the disease develops, he stands a good chance of being hospitalized for short or long terms. Even though hospital-ized, he may find his situation a desperate one. He may not be able to readjust to community life. Many schizophrenic patients have spent years of vegetating in the back wards of mental hospi-tals, forgotten not only by family and friends but also by those who practice.

This situation, of course, has changed dramatically for the better in recent years. Beginning in the mid 50s, therapeutic improvements never before possible came about with the advent of the psychoac-tive drugs. Also, there was a decline, which continues today, in the number of schizophrenic patients admitted for the first time to state and county mental hospitals and in the number of such pa-tients residing in mental hospitals. But there is still a long, long way to go. The conquest of schizophrenia has scarcely begun.

*Depression*

Another mental illness prominent among the psychoses is depres-sion. Serious disturbances in thought, behavior, and mood affect those afflicted. For some, generally the manic-depressives, there are periods of mania (elation) and depression (loss of hope, "down" feelings). They display extreme changes of mood. For others, the disorder means sustained mania, periods of continuing euphoria, excessive talk and mobility, surface happiness, and sudden dis-traught actions. For still others, the disease means depression with or without attacks of mania. A person's activities may progressively slow up. Neither he nor his family may necessarily notice this. Psychic signs begin and develop: he has difficulties in doing usual jobs: his outlook on life becomes increasingly pessimistic, and his feelings of guilt increase. Physiological difficulties also develop: he loses his appetite, and constipation sets in; he suffers from insomnia; and his physical movements become slower.

Suicide, of course, is the major danger that may result from chronic or acute attacks of depression. Most of the nation's annual toll of suicides, estimated as nearly 50,000, come from the ranks of those stricken by depression.

As with schizophrenia, the diagnosis and classification of depression is an important, unsolved problem. Here again, research and therapeutic programs to attack critical aspects of the affective disorders are increasing. There are frontal attacks upon some disorders: to prevent suicide there is a massive, progressive, nationwide program encompassing research, training of professional manpower, and services for potential suicides, such as twenty-four-hour clinics which anyone can phone or visit for help. This serves to emphasize the significance of the category of depression, as do statistics which show that, next to victims of schizophrenia, those suffering from depression occupy most mental-hospital beds. Of all patients admitted to mental institutions, around 35 percent are suffering from depression.

## NEUROSES

Neuroses—or psychoneurotic disorders—are another major category of mental illness. Although less severe than the psychoses, neuroses affect many people. The neuroses are said to have fundamental psychological causes, but there may be organic causative factors along with functional ones. The overall picture of this group of diseases is complex. Neuroses are manifested by a multitude of symptoms.

Largely, the emotional problem or problems lie in the feelings of the individual who begins to suffer from a neurosis. He may be bothered, frequently or continually, by feelings of anxiety, of awesome fears, or of depression. There may be various reactions, such as disassociation from life or environment and obsessive compulsions to do something. In specific cases, the signs and symptoms of neuroses, suggested broadly above, can be observed in individual patients such as the following:

1  A man trembling with worry about pleasing his boss becomes impossibly edgy with other workers, his family, and friends.
2  Another man turns to compulsive overeating to take his mind off his business and family problems.
3  A wife is obsessed with orderliness and having everything in place; she may fly to pieces if an ashtray on a coffee table is not precisely in line with all other objects on the table.
4  A youngster begins to walk in his sleep; he continues although nothing dangerous happens. The family more or less dismisses it. Later in life as an officer candidate, under the stress of an intensive physical and educational course, he sleepwalks and is noticed by others. He loses his chance at the cherished officer's commission and is dismissed from the armed forces as physically unfit.

There are, of course, many other neurotic patterns. They range from the tragic to the ridiculous and from the severe to the mild. Irrational fears become life-harming phobias such as endless counting or touching of objects, repeated handwashings, or the desire to step on every crack in the sidewalk.

Neuroses often have an in-and-out, up-and-down pattern. Most neurotics do not usually require hospitalization but can be professionally treated in a clinic or office during times of serious anxiety. When hospitalization is necessary, it is usually only for a brief period.

Everyone can recognize some sign, be it ever so faint, which points to some degree of neurosis in himself.

## PERSONALITY DISORDERS

Personality disorders are another type of mental illness. They are wide-ranging and heterogeneous. Also known as character disorders, they reveal themselves essentially through abnormal actions or behavior. Deviations from acceptable normal behavior patterns are the main characteristic of personality disorders. Persons suffering from personality disorders may be involved in

1 Antisocial reactions: crime, delinquency, lying, stealing, fighting, and, in general, using any means to gain their ends with no regard for the rights of others.
2 Sexual deviations: homosexuality, fetishism, transvestism; exhibitionism, voyeurism, sadism, masochism, and obsessive occupation with obscenity or pornography.
3 Drug addiction: not only addiction to narcotics (such as cocaine, heroin, opium, morphine, and other "hard" narcotics), but also addiction to or abuse of any kind of dangerous drugs (such as amphetamines, barbiturates, marihuana, LSD, and other hallucinogens).
4 Alcoholism: the alcoholic is considered to have a disordered personality.

## PSYCHOSOMATIC DISEASES

In the psychosomatic diseases, the symptoms are primarily physical, but there is a significant emotional component. The psychosomatic illnesses affect millions of sufferers through such ailments as high blood pressure, asthma, peptic ulcers, certain kinds of arthritis, colitis, and some diarrheas and headaches.

It seems sufficient here to cite the broad groups of diseases in which emotional factors play a significant role, yet in which the physical effect is primary. It is not necessary to consider signs and symptoms of the psychosomatic illnesses. The reader who desires to examine in depth the diseases mentioned should refer to specific works. The reason for this brevity here, of course, is that in these diseases the mental involvement is not considered primary. The psychosomatic disorders may be considered under such major categories as these:

1  Gastrointestinal disturbances in the appetite and in eating, in swallowing, in digestive functions, in eliminative functions.
2  Respiratory disorders such as bronchial asthma.
3  Disturbances in functions of the sexual apparatus.
4  Joint and skeletal muscle disorders such as rheumatoid arthritis and proneness toward accidents.
5  Metabolic and endocrine disturbances as found in thyrotoxicosis, fatigue states, and diabetes.
6  Skin diseases of many kinds.
7  Cardiovascular illnesses. The psychosomatic aspects of heart and blood vessel diseases are many and significant; they involve arrhythmias and tachycardia of heart action, vasopressor syncope, psychogenic headaches, and essential hypertension (or high blood pressure).

To round out the overview of the many types of mental illness, we will now look at organic brain disorders, apart from their partial inclusion in prior descriptions.

## ORGANIC BRAIN DISORDERS

Injuries and diseases may adversely affect the brain and nervous system. Any one or a combination of injuries or diseases may acutely or chronically impair the performance of the nervous system.

The causes of the processes that produce organic brain disorders are external as well as internal and include infections, trauma, tumors, toxic substances, metabolic problems, and physiological disturbances.

Considered categorically, organic brain disorders may be either acute or chronic. Acute brain disorders strike suddenly and are caused by diseases such as encephalitis, meningitis, and brain abscesses. Chronic brain disorders form an even wider range. They include congenital anomalies, multiple sclerosis, and others of what are today more commonly categorized as neurological and sensory diseases. In the main, these organic brain disorders lie largely outside the domain of mental illness itself. There is one major exception, in a sense. This is mental retardation. Involving both acute and chronic stages, this major brain-disorder problem is strongly related to many aspects of mental illness.

## Mental Retardation

Mental retardation has become recognized as a great national health problem that can be reduced, controlled, and eventually prevented through strong programs of research, treatment, and rehabilitation. Mental retardation as a body of disorders is not characterized by the strange or troubled behavior that is associated with the core mental illnesses such as psychoses and neuroses. Rather, simple or subnormal behavior and performance are displayed by the mentally retarded. These are individuals who cannot keep up with the rest of society because of some kind of intellectual deficit.

A few of the causes of mental retardation are known or suspected. Some people suffer from mental retardation as the result of an injury to the brain during birth or later in life. Another major cause of mental retardation has been early prenatal infection. The German measles virus is a familiar example of this. Blood incompatibilities between mother and child have also resulted in mental retardation in the newborn. Certain drugs and other substances taken by the prospective mother, before or during pregnancy, have been implicated.

Many things can be done to treat and prevent some kinds of mental retardation. Problems which can be solved include finding out who the mentally retarded are, to what degree they are affected, and how to provide care, treatment, and rehabilitation for them.

## PUBLIC IMAGE OF MENTAL ILLNESS

What do people in general know or believe about mental illness? What do they feel about having it? What do they believe should be done about mental illness? There have been changes for the better during the last few decades in the public's conception of mental illness and in its attitudes toward personal or community action against the problem. There is less agreement on the nature and extent of this progress and on exactly what the elements of the public image of mental illness are. The less optimistic hold that many feel great shame or revulsion when faced with mental illness either in themselves or others. Others think that these attitudes are not only less prevalent, but that public opinion is becoming more enlightened. They also feel that this improvement in public opinion will continue until mental illness is regarded as no more shameful than heart disease.

There can be little doubt that approaches to mental illness by the general public, either as individuals or as members of groups, have undergone radical change. Evidence of this lies in the research, training, and service programs that are focused against mental illness and that have been underwritten and conducted by both public and private agencies. The mental health movement was fortunate in being able to ride the post-World War II tide of public interest which resulted in massive attacks on major diseases. Such diseases as cancer, heart disease, and polio attracted enormous attention—as well as funds—and mental illness shared in this increased interest and support. The advocates of action against mental illness sought to deepen and widen public understanding of mental illness and to foster healthy attitudes toward it. This effort must have helped to fill, at least partially, some of the public's need for knowledge, but the trend toward better understanding had, of course, been underway for a good many years before.

Generally, the public has become better informed about mental illness, from having little or no information and some misinformation (say a grade of "Very Unsatisfactory") to having some information and less misinformation than earlier (say a grade of "Less Than Satisfactory, But Better Than It Was!"). Surveys and studies tend to show this and to suggest that much of the public possesses enough information to be able to act rather intelligently about mental illness. It may be, of course, that most of these people are likely to take positive action against any illness, be it stopping smoking to prevent cancer, getting periodic examinations for diabetes, or calling the physician at the first signs of what may be a strep sore throat.

The matter of public attitude can also be seen from an opposite point of view, which was a complaint voiced by the Joint Commission on Mental Illness and Health, a former agency of government and private representation that was set up by an act of Congress to study and recommend action against mental illness. Reporting in 1961 on studies sponsored by the commission and others, the agency said that the general public regarded the mentally ill with fear, distrust, and dislike. The public, according to the report, showed a wide and well-imbedded aversion to mental illness.

Nonetheless, the public does not seem to be averse to information on mental illness. The volume and kinds of inquiries—through letters, phone calls, and visits—that people make about mental

illness to all kinds of public and private agencies suggest strong
public interest, as do the programs, courses, and attention directed
to mental health/mental illness subjects in schools and colleges,
labor, industry, and civic organizations. There is also the vigorous
presentation of all aspects of mental illness via the communications
media, which makes it seem that people do want to know more
about mental illness.

# DIAGNOSIS
# & TREATMENT

## CHAPTER THREE

The process of seeking out and diagnosing victims of mental illness is different in many respects from these procedures in other fields of disease. Mental illness seems to reveal itself (though not usually in its early stages) rather than to be sought out by preventive or disease-control campaigns. X-rays can detect TB and some other lung ailments; blood tests can detect syphilis; urinalysis helps determine a diabetic; and electrocardiographs can spot certain kinds of heart disease. For the vast bulk of mental illnesses, however, there are no such tests. Another reason that they are not diagnosed as are other diseases is the still-pervasive factor of shame. There is also an element of fear which is connected with many illnesses. It keeps people from seeking lung, blood, breast, or cervical tests for cancer. But shame seems to be the main factor that conceals mental illness, makes it difficult to diagnose, and underlies public apathy.

For two major reasons—lack of diagnostic knowledge and feelings of apathy or shame—campaigns for early case finding or prevention of mental illness are not undertaken as they are in diabetes, heart disease, tuberculosis, or cancer. This is so even though it is axiomatic in mental illness, just as in organic diseases, that "the earlier found, the better and quicker helped." Perhaps we have not sufficiently encouraged ourselves to seek early attention for mental disorders. The voluntary mental-health and mental-retardation organizations, and others relating to mental and emotional diseases, do urge this. So do professional societies in psychiatry, psychology, nursing, and social work, as do the national, state, and local mental and public health agencies. But it is apparent that there is a need for more effort in the direction of early case finding and diagnosis; and it is likely that action will be taken in the next two or three decades that will parallel to some extent the massive physical disease campaigns of midcentury.

## THE NONPSYCHIATRIC PHYSICIAN

Who does diagnose mental illness? The obvious answer is "a large number of people in medical and allied professions," because several hundred thousand new cases of mental disorders are diagnosed each year. The professional disciplines are psychiatry, psychology, nursing, and social work; these, with allies in fields such as religion, jurisprudence, and education, form the core of diagnostic resources. But there is a great circle of other resources, far greater in number and in the amount of patients treated. It includes people working professionally in the health, education, and welfare field, either for themselves or for public or private agencies, but not necessarily with any specific relation to mental illness alone.

The nonpsychiatric physician is a major resource in these related groups. Physicians in specialities such as pediatrics, neurology, surgery, and cardiology can and do help diagnose—or become aware of and refer—mentally ill patients who need additional help.

But the physician in general practice sees more mental illness and can do more about it initially (upon its coming to his attention) than any other practitioner. The general practitioner (or G.P.) sees far more patients than the psychiatrist. A survey shows that one out of every seven patients who visits a G.P. has a complaint that involves a mental disorder. These complaints, a clear indication of emotional problems, include worry over the heart and blood pressure or digestive troubles. Some of the general practitioner's patients also manifest early signs of mental disease like schizophrenia or depression.

In many cases the family doctor is in the best position to make an early diagnosis, perhaps with referral to a specialist, that can lead to treatment and forestall development of the disorder into more severe stages. Alcoholism, drug abuse, and suicidal depression are symptoms of mental illness which the G.P. should be aware of. Sixty-five percent of all who commit suicide have seen a physician, usually a nonpsychiatric one, within four months of their death. These patients often show signs of depression, perhaps in demeanor or untidy dress or wild and melancholy talk. In alcoholism, an unexplained tremor, persistent facial redness, or unusual behavior or dress can tip the family doctor to the fact that a longtime patient of his is turning up with a drinking problem. The family doctor may spot the telltale signs of misuse of ordinary drugs like sleeping pills, energizers, or tranquilizers; and he generally can recognize the symptoms of narcotic drug addiction.

Most of a general practitioner's diagnostic work concerned with mental illness will not necessarily be as dramatic or as easy, however. It will entail not only his alertness, but also a good deal of routine and inevitable, but essential, paperwork. The patient, as well as the doctor, should realize this and give his full cooperation. Unfortunately, if the patient is mentally ill, in many instances he may not be able to cooperate, although he may seem to try. The wise physician knows this fact and takes it into account as he tries to diagnose not just an incidental case of sickness, but what kind of person is sick, why he is sick now, and why he has turned up with these particular symptoms. An orderly system and planned approach is made by the physician, usually employing some formal scheme of case recording, in exploring mental illness. In the doctor's file, the usual history and examination record will be built up, but with psychiatric components.

*History and Examination*

The history and physical and mental health examinations delve into many aspects of the patient's life. The doctor may ask the patient to relate in his own words what his complaint is. Rather than being laziness on the physician's part, this is a deliberate technique which can produce a useful insight into a patient's trouble. If the patient is new to the doctor, some questions about past illnesses may be asked. Similarly, if not already recorded, the patient's family history and background may be examined. His childhood and his personality prior to the current illness—or whatever brought him to the doctor—will be explored. Was he happy, nervous, shy, aggressive, afraid of the dark, robust, delicate, passive, given to fits of temper? Characteristics like these may be revealed by this technique. Sometimes these or other questions will be asked of the patient's relatives or friends who may come with him to the doctor.

The case record may also include:

> Education
>
> Delinquency
>
> Employment history
>
> Medical history: physical and psychological illnesses; if any of the latter, pertinent dates and treatment
>
> Menstrual history for women patients
>
> Marital and sexual history

Description of present illness

Recent stresses and current mental state

Along with these findings, those of the physical examination will be correlated. Besides the extensive examination from head to toe, there will be the usual tests (pulse, blood pressure, urine sample, auscultation—or "chest thumping" and listening with the stethoscope) and perhaps special tests (such as electrocardiograph, x-rays, blood sampling, or material taken for biopsy or other laboratory studies). From the results of all these investigations, which appear more formidable than they are, the physician will begin to form his judgments, taking into account other things he may know about the patient.

It is here that intangibles which cannot be precisely and adequately described come in. They involve the physician's abilities to form clinical judgments and, in the last analysis, they constitute the most important part of the diagnosis.

In any diagnosis, the G.P. can see definite psychological patterns most of the time. Through a history and examination, he can determine whether he should treat the patient himself or refer him to a specialist, a psychiatrist, or a psychiatric clinic.

## THE PSYCHIATRIST

Generally, the specialist is not out looking for the mentally ill; he has as many as he can handle. But there is a developing trend, the practice of community psychiatry, in which the psychiatrist and the community are interacting with each other and seeking to help more and more of the mentally ill. Through community mental health centers, psychiatric hospitals, private and public clinics, and other agencies, the specialist and the groups seeking to find and help the mentally disordered are in a sense case finding, as is the physician in general practice when he refers a patient to a psychiatrist. When a patient is referred, there are many sophisticated approaches which may be used by the specialist. As he seeks to form an evaluation and an eventual diagnosis, the psychiatrist will draw upon the background that has already been evolved. But he will also be likely to institute additional procedures of a highly detailed, refined, and comprehensive nature.

## Psychiatric History and Examination

Brief highlights will serve to illustrate the psychiatric approach to diagnosis and some of the methods employed. Requiring a high degree of psychiatric skills, the examination depends especially upon the psychiatrist. But there is often also involved, directly or indirectly, a skilled team: for example, that of the psychologist (for tests and evaluations), the nurse (for office or home help), and the social worker (for family-history assistance, casework, and environmental information). The examination also requires that the fullest possible information be obtained concerning the patient with respect to all these factors: chemical, anatomical, physiological, social, environmental, familial, psychological, and educational status, past and present. This mammoth task may never be completed to perfection, but its undertaking yields valuable information; and it can never be predicted in advance which factors will turn up revealing clues and key evidence.

What are some of the elements of the psychiatric history? It will contain components of the history discussed previously which the alert, informed general practitioner takes. It will be different, however, and will differ among specialists according to the particular approach of each, though in degree rather than in kind.

This is expected. Psychiatry is not an exact science; and it has no precise and absolute diagnostic formulas. But neither do other fields. Cardiovascular surgery, though much more susceptible to exactitude than psychiatry, contains both subtle and gross variations in its theories and techniques. This is not said in apology for psychiatry, which is sometimes and probably unfairly said to lag 150 years behind medical-health fields. Rather it is mentioned to point out that the psychiatric history and examination properly offer many variations on common, and unusual, themes. What is presented here does not comprehend either any one or all schools of psychiatric thought. It represents current trends to find out what may be wrong with the individual suspected, either by himself or by others, of being mentally ill.

## The Psychiatric History

Almost invariably, the psychiatric history begins with basic facts about the patient: name, age, sex, address, occupation. Then it may proceed to the reasons for the visit and an examination. Did the patient himself decide to come in? Was he referred by another physician? Was he referred by a social agency, school, or other organization? Or is he being required by a court of law to be examined for purposes of determining whether or not he should be committed to a hospital or, perhaps, undergo psychiatric treatment in an outpatient clinic? A statement of the problem may follow in the patient's own words. He will be encouraged to say what he himself thinks is wrong.

A detailed account of the development of the current episode of sickness is prepared. In addition, other things will be detailed, including the patient's biological functions such as sleeping, eating, bowel and bladder function, drinking, drug-taking, and sexual activities. The reasons will be sought for the patient's visit at the particular time and indications of previous attacks, if any, of mental illness.

The family history will be recorded, including information on the patient's genetic, economic, familial, and social environment; on the relationships and customs of parents, siblings, and others in the home; and on whether there is or has been mental illness, alcoholism, narcotic addiction, or abnormal behavior among others of the family.

Delving into personal history, the psychiatrist will seek facts and impressions about each period of the patient's life: infancy, childhood, adolescence, adulthood, and old age. In connection with his personality, description and evaluation of his activities and characteristics will be prepared, along with information on especially disturbing emotional experiences.

The psychiatrist will use laboratory tests to gather information also, calling on hospital or general medical laboratories to perform examinations of the composition of the blood, urine, and if necessary, spinal fluid. Liver-function tests, glandular studies, and x-rays of the skull, lungs, and spine may be employed. He may well have electroencephalographs taken. This is the recording of certain electrical impulses of the brain to establish brain-wave patterns. The test is made with electrodes attached, in much the same manner as the taking of electrocardiographs—electrical impulses—of the heart. Although the practical value of the electroencephalograph has not yet been fully determined, the instrument appears to be of some use. Its major role has been as a research tool, but considerable study of its clinical implications has been involved. Like many other instrumentation developments, the electroencephalograph will probably be clinically useful even if it is not of tremendous diagnostic value.

The psychiatrist will require the patient to have a physical examination, as it is an indispensable part of the psychiatric study. Some of the tools and tests have already been mentioned; others even more familiar will be included: the stethoscope, electrocardiograph, reflex hammer, and sphygmomanometer (blood pressure gauge).

*The Psychiatric Examination*

The psychiatric examination involves twenty or more categories of careful psychological analysis of the patient. This examination will include such subjects as general appearance and attitude; consciousness; affectivity, thought processes and content; perception; memory; judgment; insight; and maturity of personality.

Various tests such as the following may be used:

> Wechsler Adult Intelligence Scale
>
> Personality tests
>
> Thematic Aperception Test
>
> Bender Gestalt Test
>
> Draw-A-Person test
>
> Sentence Completions Test
>
> Minnesota Multiphasic Personality Inventory
>
> Rorschach inkblot test

Rorschach's inkblot test not only is illustrative of the psychological-test field, but also is among the best known of psychological tests. It is one of the more interesting tests and is considered to have widest applicability. It does, however, present difficulties of interpretation and require an experienced physician or psychologist to administer and to evaluate. Such a person can draw useful conclusions from the Rorschach test concerning the patient's personality, character, intelligence, and symptoms of illness.

The batteries of psychological tests and the trained interpretive skills of psychologists constitute a valuable and indispensable component of the whole study of the patient and work toward the formulation of the best possible diagnosis. Psychological tests can help determine and establish many facts about the basic personality patterns of the patient. But they are *not* diagnostic procedures in themselves, and they should not be so considered. The extent of psychological contributions to the whole study depends upon the skills and relationships of the psychologist and psychiatrist and their mutual recognition of what tests and other measures can and cannot achieve. Well employed, psychology contributes invaluable work in evaluation of intellectual functions, organic brain damage, personality, suitability of psychotherapy, and chances of recovery.

The wealth of information resulting from the entire diagnostic study is a storehouse of psychiatric findings; and the fuller and better the inventory, the surer and better the likelihood that a useful diagnosis will be formulated. After a specific diagnosis has been made and the patient's illness has been classified, this is not the end. It is but the beginning—for the truly important question that next has to be asked and answered is; What do we do about this person's treatment?

## TREATMENT

No one theory or method of diagnosis or treatment can be called superior; no one system can be followed exclusively. The need for an open-door policy is indicated, using the best of the old or current approaches and trying new ways as well. This policy was the conclusion of the most authoritative investigation of mental illness in this country in this century, published in 1961 by the Joint Commission on Mental Illness and Health.

There are a thousand therapies (not including 10 times 10,000 quackeries) to bring a person back to mental health from mental illness—or, better yet, to keep him mentally healthy. We will not consider the billion-dollar business of quackeries. It is difficult enough to encompass understandably the approved measures used to treat mental illness and sustain mental health. These measures may be grouped into manageable arrangements. Psychotherapy, in all its variations, is the method most used in the management and treatment of cases of mental illness. Let us now appraise favored means of treatment.

Some therapies are interdependent, and others overlap so that in effect there is no single isolated method. If we try to divide treatment into organic and psychological, we immediately run into difficulty. Most therapies have characteristics of other classes, and frequent intermixings of therapy are common. Nevertheless, we can establish groupings for certain classes of treatment.

Psychoanalysis

Psychotherapy

Psychotherapy and other means

Drug therapy

Social therapy

Physical and shock therapies

Now let us examine these various treatments.

## Psychoanalysis

The term *psychoanalysis* was devised by Freud for his new and theoretical system of therapy. In the years since the term was coined its meaning has changed. *Psychoanalysis* means more in that the original concept has been analyzed and extended by interpreters (including both believers and nonbelievers) into a larger universe of theory than perhaps Freud himself ever dreamed of. The term means less in that psychoanalytic treatment is not as widely employed as it once was. Also, spinoffs and innovative therapies—aimed at more immediate and practical returns than psychoanalysis—have proliferated in recent years.

Psychoanalysis may be defined as a psychological system using the Freudian hypothesis of the unconscious: there is a part of the mind which does not operate consciously. Psychoanalytic methods involve freeing the patient's unconscious by having him—while reclining on the familiar couch or in a comfortable chair—unburden himself of feelings and thoughts by talking, by relating anything that comes to his mind.

The psychiatrist, through this free-association outpouring of words, listens, notes, and interprets with the principles of psychoanalysis in mind (i.e., that the patient will resist and then will transfer feelings and hostilities to the physician for a time; and that the patient's dreams have meaning and must be elucidated and analyzed). The analyst's role is to help the patient to recognize the unconscious feelings that have played a part in his troubles. Gaining such insight may provide relief for the patient.

Psychoanalysis has helped patients with some kinds of mental illness, notably certain neuroses. But it has not been effective against the major mental disorders of schizophrenia and manic depression. Psychoanalysis has other limitations. For one, it requires many months to be effectively implemented. An analysis will often extend over one, two, or more years. There have been and are efforts to modify and shorten the psychoanalytic process. In the main, these efforts have been experimental and have not been adopted. Psychoanalysis also requires intensive time and attention on the part of the psychiatrist. He must be qualified in the theory and practice of psychoanalysis as a therapeutic method. Far from all psychiatrists are either skilled or desirous of devoting themselves in this kind of practice.

Of the millions of people in the United States who are treated for mental illness each year, only a small fraction can or will be treated by psychoanalysis. This is not to say that the technique has gone out of favor or use or that it is likely to disappear. Besides, it is useful in research as a method for scientific investigations in normal and abnormal personality.

*Psychotherapy*

*Psychotherapy* means, simply, the nursing or cure or treatment of the spirit or mind. *Therapy* comes from the Greek *therapia*, "to nurse," and *psycho*, comes from the Greek *psyche*, "mind" or "spirit."

*Psychotherapy* is the most generic term in mental illness treatment, although most authorities do not classify everything under it, but make various groupings. It may be in the future that, if there is just one mental illness, as some authorities assert, there will be just one treatment—whether or not it will be called psychotherapy. The term has long since gone into the vernacular and has attained popular usage: "He psyched me into going along with him." If the "psyching" was tried in order to help the person with an emotional or mental problem, it was an attempt at psychotherapy, albeit unprofessional and, chances are, more damaging than helpful.

Professionally, almost any method employed by a general physician, psychiatrist, or clinical team to help a person to adjust better to life and to remove or ameliorate his emotional or mental problem's effects may be psychotherapy. It has been called the art and science of treating mental and emotional disease through changing ideas and emotions in order to bring about a more favorable psychic equilibrium. This definition is probably broad enough for most purposes, and it encompasses a host of methodologies. Among them are

> Persuasion
>
> Hypnosis
>
> Confession, reassurance, encouragement, approval
>
> Bibliotherapy (the use of reading)

*Psychotherapy Plus*

Strictly speaking, *psychotherapy* means using only psychological means to treat an illness. There is no patent on the method, and nonpsychiatrists, of course, often employ psychological measures when treating physical ailments.

When organic or physical means are used in mental illness treatment by psychotherapists, the therapy becomes something else.

Ordinarily, this means using drugs as well as psychological techniques such as persuasion, reassurance, and suggestion. It can, of course, mean using special diets or physical exercise generally supportive of the psychotherapy or using other components of the patient's environment. These kinds of treatment and those employing drugs are the two major trends of the present times. They may well turn out to be the major achievements of the twentieth century in combatting mental illness. Whatever their future, they deserve fairly detailed description. They will simply be called, for convenience's sake, *drug therapy* and *social therapy.*

## Drug Therapy

The use of plant, mineral, or animal extracts and compounds for medicinal purposes is as old as mankind. That the purpose of some of the earliest drugs used by man was to affect the mind and spirit seems also probable.

At midcentury in our times came the revolutionary explosion of the so-called mind drugs and the breakthrough of drug therapy for mental illness. Since then, many of the principal drugs coming to professional and public attention have been the psychoactive (psychopharmacological) drugs—substances used for their mental effects. Though not fully understood nor tested, these drugs have proved beyond doubt to be of vast significance in the treatment of mental illness and in supporting mental health. They have already indisputably become major clinical tools for the treatment, supportively if not specifically, of nearly all kinds of mental illness. They are also invaluable research tools for brain-chemistry studies in animals and man. Such studies will help determine their real place and significance in mental illness and health. They are confronting us with the staggering realization that there now exist, or can be created, powerful new compounds which have the potential of drastically and profoundly altering—no one today can be sure whether for better or for worse—either our minds or our bodies or both.

The mammoth developments in drugs and the startling potentialities of genetic modeling and other means to produce superbrains (or the reverse, subhumans) give emphasis to the need for research in all aspects of the life sciences. Full understanding of how to use future technology must be attained in drugs as in many other fields. Otherwise, man as we now know him could soon disappear from the earth, certainly in less time than the several million years it took to make him what he is today.

Descending from high speculative planes, we find that the rational use of drugs for mental health and against mental illness is, as might be suspected, in its scientific infancy. Mind drugs may figure in every third or fourth drugstore prescription, but they are given and taken more on faith than upon specificity. Yet there can be little quarrel with the thesis that they do much good; and few would want to turn back the clock and do away with all our modern mind drugs.

Modern psychoactive drug therapy has its roots in the nineteenth century, when rational approaches to study and use of drugs were sought. The beginnings of psychopharmacology, the study of the nature and properties of drugs that produce mental effects, were laid then. Today's mind drugs began in about 1953. First, phenothiazines, with chlorpromazine were introduced. These were followed closely by compounds derived from a plant *Rauwolfia serpentina*, growing on the slopes of the Himalayas. These compounds were first used in the United States to lower blood pressure.

These major drugs and their derivatives and analogs were called tranquilizers, because their principal effect was a calming one. With two other main groups, the diphenylmethanes and the propenediols, they constitute the bulk of the therapeutically prescribed tranquilizing drugs, though there are many other kinds of substances which produce calming effects. These four categories of tranquilizers are prescribed by general physicians and psychiatrists.

They are widely and heavily used and are found under various pharmaceutical company brand names. For each of the four classes, there are several similar products produced by several drug houses.

Commercial research—both basic and clinical—is diligently pursued by industry, and a great deal of drug research is also supported by government and universities in seeking not only more ideal mind drugs, but also new drugs for cancer and heart disease.

In addition to the tranquilizers, there are two other categories of therapeutic drugs: the antidepressants or psychic energizers, particularly the amphetamines, and the sedative or sleep-assisting agents, such as the barbiturates. Sometimes called the up-and-down drugs, these pep pills and sleeping pills are also widely used as adjunctive therapy in various kinds of mental illness. As with the tranquilizers, they also are manufactured under various brand names by pharmaceutical companies, and they are available only upon prescription. But unfortunately this has not prevented their wide abuse any more than for the tranquilizers.

It should be strongly pointed out, in considering the use of drugs in mental illness treatment, that none of them will produce cures, that none should be taken without medical prescription and supervision, and that none is without risk. This by no means discounts the tremendous importance and value of these drugs. They have had a momentous impact upon medicine, including psychiatry, in its treatment of the mental patient. Their most revolutionary achievement has been in the results of their use in mental hospitals. The final report to the U.S. Congress of the Joint Commission on Mental Illness and Health, established by the Congress to recommend action upon the problem of mental illness, after its five-year study came to the conclusion in 1961 that the tranquilizers have revolutionized the management of psychotic patients in American mental hospitals and probably deserve primary credit for reversal of the upward spiral of the state-hospital inpatient load. Debate is still under way, however, as to precisely what the drugs accomplish physiologically and socially. The use of these drugs in and out of hospitals continues, as does a yearly decline of mental patients in public mental hospitals. Far from being written, therefore, is the ultimate word on chemical therapy. Further revolutions may be looked for, based perhaps on some of the drugs mentioned here or on other nondrugs, such as vitamins, which are also used but not widely, or on compounds yet to be discovered. We can be sure that drug therapy is here to stay and to grow.

## Social Therapy

The treatment of patients as social beings rather than as isolated individuals stems from the "moral treatment" of Pinel and the purveyors of modern humanitarianism. They regard mental illness as a sickness of community significance rather than as willful wrongdoing or the result of evil spirits.

As a term, *social therapy* is most meaningful and useful as a means of including in one category some of the many new methodologies of treatment. It is convenient to describe these new methodologies as subcategories of a social movement evolved from psychotherapy as it originally was. Then therapy was chiefly a matter of a one-to-one relationship between a healer and a sick person. Furthermore, therapy was directed toward the amelioration of his trouble and not toward the whole man or the involvement of his community.

Only brief glimpses of a few of the prominent new therapies are given here. All these theories are experimental and await full evaluation. Among the ways and means to a golden end are these society-oriented approaches: group, family, hospital, psychodrama, milieu, and community therapies.

## Group Therapy

Group therapy, essentially simple in definition, refers to the treatment of several patients at one time in a group. Group therapy has been used in connection with organic diseases also. In the early 1900s it was used with patients suffering form tuberculosis; and a similar group treatment of this kind may be seen in sessions and clubs arranged for cancer patients and coronary heart attack victims. The use of this method has spread widely since World War II, principally as an encouraging, practical, and useful way to handle and help the mentally ill. One reason for its large increase is that it offered perhaps the only way to treat more of the vast number of patients when there were only a handful of therapists.

There have never been, and probably never will be, enough trained physicians and other therapists to treat every mental patient on a one-to-one basis adequately and over a period of time. But expediency is far from the only reason for group therapy. More valid reasons are found in its nature, usually well accepted by patients and professionals, its bringing people together to share problems and gains, and specific indications of its need (as for patients who strongly shun individual therapy).

The makeup of groups meeting for psychotherapy is determined by the nature of the patients' illnesses and their needs; the patients who are selected and the particular methods that are used by the therapist will depend upon what illnesses are manifested in a group. How group therapy is organized and conducted varies widely. Ordinarily, it is characterized by factors such as comfortable environment, regular sessions, the therapist serving as catalyst, permissiveness of verbal expression, lack of unnecessary restrictions, an hour or an hour-and-a-half meeting once a week, and uninhibited critical evaluation of reaction to group interactions.

Because of its promise and popularity, group therapy is receiving considerable research exploration. Several schools of thought have developed with a wide range of systems, from free-association, or analytical, to educational and directed clinical approaches aimed at reducing abnormal behavior symptoms. Group therapy has not been proved conclusively to be as successful as all early hopes held it might be. The technique does seem to be effective in many cases and is currently growing. One encouraging example is its use with groups of senile oldsters, with helpful results. Since the term *group therapy*, is somewhat generic, all the social therapies are involved. They owe tribute or their origin to group therapy.

## Family Therapy

Family therapy involves a clinical approach in which a child, an adolescent, or an adult with mental illness is treated for his emotional disorder under the concept that there is something in the family relationships which has caused or helped cause the illness. The therapist studies the whole family and their psychological dynamics, their social and cultural setting, and involves them all in the therapy. Treatment is thus family-oriented. In a way, the family is itself the patient. The person who has come to attention as mentally ill is indicative of a family illness.

The aims of family therapy are to create understanding among family members, to improve their relationships with each other, and to help the sick member by achieving a mentally healthy family environment as well as by administering to his individual needs. The therapist, bringing the family together and serving as a catalyst in implementing harmonious relationships, encourages them to talk with each other rather than to him, which often happens in early sessions. In the process of face-to-face interchange, members of the family learn to communicate more fully, to recognize causes of conflict better, and to find ways of reducing their conflicts.

Family therapy is a formidable, difficult technique; it is not useful in all kinds of mental illness nor for all families; and the therapist has to select most carefully those who will become his "patient family." Relatively new (having been conceived of about 1950), family therapy is the subject of a good deal of research as well as of clinical use.

*Hospital Therapy*

The treatment of mental illness in a hospital setting can be effective if the patient is not merely given custodial care, as used to be almost universally true and still is too often the case. Every patient admitted to a mental hospital or to the psychiatric ward of a general hospital requires meaningful therapy. This would seem obvious, but it is a recent and not yet completely accepted belief. The modern philosophy is that psychotherapy and measures supporting it are necessary and should be focused intensively upon the patient's condition.

Just as would be done if the patient were in the hospital for an appendectomy, the facility's attention is directed toward removing his difficulty and returning him to home as soon as possible. Modern trends in hospital treatment include all the categories and subcategories of therapy mentioned earlier, plus many others such as psychodrama, recreational and occupational therapy, music and art therapy, foster homes, halfway houses, and sheltered workshops. Part-time hospitalization is another recent development of magnitude, not only in the United States but also abroad. Under this practice, a patient may spend either the day, or some part of it, or the night in the hospital. He travels back and forth freely to work or to his home. While at the hospital, he receives an appropriate treatment such as group therapy.

*Milieu Therapy*

*Milieu* means one's surroundings or environment. *Milieu therapy* means nursing or curing mental illness by means of manipulating the patient's environment. This is a simple concept with many implications. The patient is treated in relation to his total environment. Its components, including work, play, sleeping, eating, and other facilities, are put to use by a therapeutic team of health workers who manipulate them to help the patient. Many experimental programs—particularly in hospital settings—are developing and evaluating milieu therapy.

## Community Therapy

Since the 1950s, the most dramatic development in mental health has been the rapid rise and spread of community therapy. To a certain degree community therapy is simultaneously the outgrowth of psychiatrists' response to social needs by moving out into their communities and the manifestation of the community's desire to get involved in the matter of mental health.

Community psychiatry has been held to be a subspecialty of psychiatry which focuses on the prevention, diagnosis, treatment, and rehabilitation of emotional illness and their consequences in a given population. Community psychiatry, therefore, aims its efforts not at an individual, but rather at the total community population and high-risk or high-need components of that population, such as disturbed children.

To say that community therapy is a psychiatric subspecialty means that this technique utilizes methods not necessarily new to the psychiatrist, but also not necessarily the kind of methods he is comfortable with or knows much about. These methods include social planning, cooperative consultation, and cooperative public education. In fortunate communities, there used to be few community-oriented private psychiatrists and perhaps one working full or part time in a health agency clinic who were involved in what was, in part at least, community psychiatry. The trend, once begun, continued and grew with the involvement of more professionals and community agencies such as medical clinics and welfare groups. The concept arose that these individuals and agencies working together could provide the community with comprehensive mental health services to meet all the people's needs.

When the question arose concerning whether anyone other than the psychiatrist practiced community psychiatry, the answer was apparent. Obviously, it was not his sole domain. Nor did the enlightened psychiatrist wish it so. Obviously, such people as nurses, social workers, psychologists, educators, clergymen, policemen, judges, epidemiologists, and volunteers were helping in the practice of community psychiatry. We have used the term *community psychiatry*, or *community therapy*, as an umbrella to cover this new approach, which is actually only a revision of the community mental health program.

There are, however, so many new facets to this approach that it has become an entirely different program rather than merely being a change in degree from the traditional community health program. This was given national expression in 1963 when President Kennedy called for a "bold new approach" to the mental illness problem of our community of states. The President proposed that the old journey to massive mental institutions be abandoned. Instead, he urged that the total needs of all people facing mental and emotional diseases be met through the development of services that are adequate and accessible to anyone regardless of race, creed, or financial status. These services had to be organized to identify and to satisfy the entire spectrum of needs, in contrast to the old way of providing hospitals where certain mentally sick would receive mere custody or partial treatment.

This message heralded the revolution in mental illness that is now in progress and from which are evolving a vast nationwide network of community mental health centers and other services. Since these are programmatic rather than specific treatment methods, they are presented in a subsequent chapter. But they do form the framework and much of the covering of what is termed community therapy.

## Physical-Shock Therapies

To round out this short survey of the many therapies for mental illness, we will look at three physical methods of treatment: electric shock, insulin-coma shock, and psychosurgery. These rather bizarre treatments appear to be falling from favor; certainly the popularity they once enjoyed is waning.

Electroconvulsive therapy, sometimes called *ECT*, is carried out by giving a patient a series of electric shocks, each consisting of from 80 to 100 volts. He has uncontrollable convulsions and is rendered unconscious. This treatment is designed to relieve depression by temporarily impairing memory.

Insulin-coma shock treatment, which predates electric shock although both rose in the 1930s, produces somewhat similar effects. It has been used chiefly with patients suffering from schizophrenia. Combinations of insulin coma and electric shock have also been employed.

Another drastic physical attack upon mental illness has been the surgical procedure known as prefrontal lobotomy. This involves surgically cutting brain fibers for the purpose of controlling abnormal behavior and emotions. It has been claimed that this calms highly excited, uncontrollable patients, but also that it reduces them to a vegetable-like state.

With the advent of the psychoactive drugs, which helped achieve far more simply, safely, surely, and cheaply many of the results sought by drastic physical shock therapies, these therapies have receded. As the final report of the Joint Commission on Mental Illness and Health said in 1961 about the psychoactive drugs: "They have largely replaced the various forms of shock, as well as surgery on the prefrontal lobes of the brain [lobotomy]." Nothing has happened since 1961 to do other than reinforce that statement.

## OUTLOOK

The earlier that diagnosis is made and necessary treatment is begun, the better are the chances of full recovery. This has been found to be true of mental disorders as it is of most physical diseases. New programs of community mental health services which seeks to provide early detection and case finding, although now in their infancy, offer great promise for the future.

The outlook for those patients whose illness requires hospitalization is increasingly hopeful, with shorter lengths of stay required for many patients and improved hospital services and therapies. Mental illness is, nonetheless, often a chronic illness. Just as in most other chronic illnesses, there will be periods of remission and recurrence, in which further treatment is necessary. This should be no more a cause for despair than are the problems of chronic diseases such as rheumatic fever or diabetes. The fact that these and other chronic diseases can be controlled, if not eradicated, by modern therapy such as drugs, is well known. The fact that many cases of mental illness can also be managed ought to be equally well known.

Treatments for rheumatic fever and diabetes have shown continued improvement over the past years and continue to do so; such is also the case with mental illness. Many authorities hold not only that the treatment of mental illness will continue to improve, but also that biochemical, genetic, or other breakthroughs in the not too distant future will bring near conquests of some mental illnesses. It has been speculated, for instance, that the biological approach to schizophrenia might develop a treatment as effective for this major mental disorder as penicillin has been for early syphilis.

# WHAT IS MENTAL HEALTH?

CHAPTER FOUR

We have considered some of the difficulties in determining what mental illness is. The definitions for both *mental illness* and *mental health* are illusive, making it, at times, very difficult to draw a line between the two. Behavior that is abnormal at one time may be acceptable at another. What may be one man's meat, as the old saw goes, is another man's poison. What one society approves and condones, another will censure and punish. Any one of us might seem mentally ill to a man from a primitive culture. On the other hand, if primitives who practised polyandry came to the United States to live, we would not consider their practice mentally healthy.

Comparisons are only part of the story. Yet, if we do not know what mental illness is, how can we know what constitutes mental health? As pointed out earlier in summarizing the opinions about mental illness, an enormous amount of effort throughout the ages has been directed at definition and classification. The continuum remains one of confusion, disagreement, and disorder, although psychiatry somehow struggles through with sucess in diagnosing and defining certain cases. A number of major modern works in the field of psychiatry and mental illness have little to say about mental health, prevention of mental illness, or community psychiatry. Trying to define and classify mental health has always required less effort than the search for disease identification has. There are some signs, however, that the scales are tipping, for in recent years discussions and literature concerning mental health have increased considerably. Mental health in its own right has now attained a great deal of professional attention.

The apostles of mental health are certain that there *is* such a state of being; and they valiantly attempt to define mental health; but their efforts are too often as verbose as they are brave. They feel, moreover, with some reason, that mental health (or mental illness, for that matter) is too important to be left entirely to physicians. However great their prolixity and however unsure their attempts to define mental health from the medical sciences' standpoint, there is a point here in paraphrasing Voltaire: "If mental health did not exist, it would be necessary to invent it."

But the dichotomy that exists between the fighters of mental illness and the seekers of mental health is ordinarily a friendly one. The mental health promoters come primarily from the ranks of psychology, social work, education, liberal arts, and plain do-goodism, but the practical clinicians, who usually have the most to do with the difficult business of treating the mentally ill, are also concerned. Basically, the curious but understandable fact that health is infinitely harder to define than disease is always involved.

## HEALTH / ILLNESS

From the earliest of times, more has been written about disease than about health. Perhaps this is because health does not challenge us, while disease—or illness—does. Health and illness are like peace and war; we pay less attention to the "peace" of health than we do to the "war" of illness. "I'm feeling good," you say to yourself, "why should I worry?" While we are feeling good, we do not think much about health; but our attitude changes when disease strikes us or someone we know. Then disease becomes a personal challenge, an affront, an insult, an onslaught.

When you are sick or when someone close to you is sick, you think longingly of health. You wish that you could be well again or that you could help your friend to feel better. You think about disease and death as well as health and life. These four words—*life* and *health, disease* and *death*—are among the great ideas with which man concerns himself. Coming to grips with these four ideas is immensely difficult. Health is a barrier between life and disease; although life can exist with disease, disease is the vanguard of eventual death. Thus, on one end of the scale is life, and on the other, death. Life and death appear then to be natural enemies. This also may be the case for health and disease; for life and death are separated by health and disease. Consider the word *life*. Nobody knows precisely what life is. It seems to be many things that distinguishes an animal or plant from "dead" or inanimate things. Life shows chemical changes, growth, aging, reproduction, and powers of adaptation to its environment. Life is also a "vital force," that is, a living power—which is almost to say that *life* is *life*.

It is also difficult to define *health*. Health has been called a "state of being hale or sound in body, mind, or soul; especially, freedom from disease or pain." But to say that *health* means "hale" is to say that *health* means "health." A medical dictionary definition is not of much help, either, saying that health is "A normal condition of body or mind."

It is easier to define *disease*. *Disease* stems from the Latin word *aise* meaning "ease." *Disease* means literally "the absence of comfort." Yet a great deal more than lack of ease lies underneath.

Cancer is a disease, but it is much more than the mere absence of ease.

In this era of organ transplants, there is a more urgent need for a definition of death. But, as with life, nobody knows exactly what death is. In the popular mind, death is the opposite of life. One medical definition is that death is the "cessation or extinction of life."

Man knows, on the whole, more about health and disease than about life and death. He knows how to attack disease successfully. This is precisely the point that clinicians (particularly those who are physicians) are likely to make in most discussions of mental health. They see mental health as a goal to be sought through a multitude of difficulties, perhaps a sort of pilgrim's progress past the great slough of despond (depression) and other obstacles. Theirs is a straight-line approach, going back to Hippocrates, in which harmony is sought as a delicate but achievable balance between the various forces and influences of the mind and body. You treat and cure or ameliorate mental disease and, ergo, you have mental health.

Mental health, it is conceded, stems from the fullest possible understanding of one's own motivations and actions; this concept is Freudian in origin. Mental health, the clinicians say, is the attainment of mental well-being by the early prevention of emotional disorders and, when these have occurred, through secondary preventive measures—detection, treatment, and rehabilitation of the mentally sick.

## PREVENTION OF MENTAL ILLNESS

Many adherents to this view would hasten to add that primary prevention is generally unattainable and that we do well enough to wrestle with secondary prevention. This means trying to reduce the amount and incidence of mental disorders by finding, treating, and returning to useful life the greatest possible number of those people who are mentally ill.

Primary and secondary measures, singly or together, have both succeeded and failed in movements aimed at other kinds of man's major illnesses. I will not go into these methods in depth, but it might be said that most of these have neither completely succeeded nor completely failed. Rheumatic fever, for instance, has long been a subject of both primary- and secondary-prevention campaigns. Primary work is aimed at prompt, effective antibiotic treatment which can eradicate streptococcal infections which precede rheumatic fever. Secondary prophylaxis (disease prevention and control) prevents recurring attacks of rheumatic fever through long-term use of antibiotics or sulphonamides. The work has enjoyed its successes and setbacks, but the consensus has been that the former outweigh the latter. The substantial death-rate decline may have resulted in part from the programs against rheumatic fever and rheumatic heart disease.

Such endeavors against disease suggest that mental health, although an illusive thing, is a practical goal to be sought through an attack on mental illness. Many of those now concerned with the field would feel this way, though their philosophies and approaches would not necessarily be in agreement.

Yet there still exists the dichotomy mentioned in 1961 in the final report of the Joint Commission on Mental Illness and Health. The commission found that there were two national movements. One advocated mental health advancement and the other encouraged mental illness treatment. The commission's conclusion seemed to be that it was futile, or nearly so, to attempt to promote mental health when so little attempt had been made to solve the problem of mental illness. Furthermore, the commission held that we had not done all that was possible concerning mental disorders themselves.

The debates about concepts and practices continue as they do in other fields of health and in other aspects of man's community life. But there has been a growing partnership, in practice if not in philosophy. There *is* a march toward the goal of mental health, wherever it is, whatever it may be.

Some of the mental health definitions developed by the joint commission's studies are noteworthy. The purpose of the studies was to analyze the concept of positive mental health, particularly from the psychological point of view. The studies reflected the then growing and now even more burgeoning incursion of the behavioral sciences into mental health. The thesis was advanced that positive mental health requires focus not only on sick behavior but also on human behavior as a normal phenomenon. The commission's studies of the concepts of mental health then current presented interesting ideas, as the following examples show.

Mental health, the studies held, is an individual and personal matter; and, although environment may be involved in the causes of mental illness, the illness is an individual characteristic that does not necessarily indicate a "sick society" or a "sick community." Another conclusion was that standards of mentally healthy, or normal, behavior vary with the time, place, culture, and expectations of the social group; that is, different peoples have different standards.

The studies found that mental health is one of many human values, and it should not be regarded as the ultimate good in itself. It was also concluded that no completely acceptable, all-inclusive concept existed for physical health or physical illness, and, likewise, none existed for mental health or mental illness. The studies, besides crystallizing many views, pointed out the need for more intensive scientific research in mental health.

Since these concepts about mental health were expressed, there have been major program innovations rather than conceptual changes. Targeted toward the goal of mental health improvement for all, there is a common theme among these concepts: many means can and must be used for the prevention of mental illness.

The program of nationwide community mental health centers is an expression of the need for and practicality of both primary and secondary prevention. On the debit side of the ledger can be placed facts like these: far from all that can be done toward the prevention of mental illness is being done; there are many limitations to what even the most comprehensive prevention programs can accomplish; and it is impossible to evaluate with scientific accuracy what is being accomplished through prevention activities which, after all, are extremely costly. There is one inescapable fact, however, that establishes the position reached on prevention. There are many mental illness disorders about which enough is known—imperfect though that knowledge may be—about causes, nature, and treatment to qualify them for local, state, and national attack through planned programs.

Some known cases of mental illness are not being treated at all, and some are being inadequately treated. There are not enough psychiatrists and other trained personnel to take care of these cases, and certainly not enough to seek out new people to help. There are not even enough facilities for known needs. Grant that these facts are true. Grant also that undertaking prevention programs may cause demands for services to far outnumber the supply. But it cannot be granted that this is reason to do nothing but grind along on the basis of "Let's take care of what we can handle and not turn up new problems."

## COMMUNITY MENTAL HEALTH

The die has already been cast. Its most dramatic result in the United States was the passage of the Community Mental Health Centers Act by Congress in 1963. This act provides for a nationwide network of mental health centers with comprehensive services—a major thrust of which involves preventive programs. The act and the network of several hundred centers in local communities are testimony to the fact that overrides the many reasons advanced for postponing prevention endeavors: enough means are already at hand to effect progress. This does not mean abandonment of traditional therapeutic methods or the psychiatric hospital or good psychiatric care in general hospitals or the individual patient-to-therapist relationship. Rather, current preventive efforts seek to complement and supplement such techniques.

But what are some of the areas of promise for preventive programs? On mental illnesses resulting from physical illnesses, defects, or injuries, there is much to be desired. Mental deficiency in children is strongly associated in many instances with the mother-to-be having had German measles in the first three months of her pregnancy; other viral diseases have also been implicated. Drugs taken by the expectant mother are also of danger to the child, as are nutritional diseases during pregnancy. The effective treatment or prevention of these and other physiological illnesses can then play a great role in prevention of mental illness.

Then there is the major bulk of mental disorders, schizophrenia, depression, and other mental and emotional problems which may be less severe or less prevalent but nevertheless are a grave burden. Yet there is hope through prevention here, too. A major example may be the development of consultation and education services, especially in areas where there are community mental health centers, as a new mental health tool. The technique, in oversimplified terms, is to help people such as professionals in various local agencies to help potential or early victims of mental illness.

Thousands can be saved from severe mental or emotional suffering by being helped through crises or by learning positive ways to handle stressful situations. Thousands of others are unable to function at their full capacity or lead satisfying, productive lives. "The untreated sick, the potentially ill, and all those whose potential for better health is undeveloped represent a vast accumulation of unmet needs which can now be met at community levels," says the National Institute of Mental Health concerning the preventive activities of community mental health centers.

The consultation and education technique has been defined. Consultation is considered a two-way process. It is a systematic use of mental health knowledge to achieve the greatest good for the greatest number. Generally, it means a voluntary relationship between two or more professional people to exchange information and to collaborate on solving an existing or potential mental health problem. The consultant is always a mental health specialist. He or she may be a psychiatrist, a psychologist, a psychiatric social worker, a mental health nurse, or a community worker with special mental health training. The consultee is usually from a community agency, which may be either a public or private health organization. It may be the school system, the police department, or a business, labor, religious, or civic group. The client is the person, group, or system helped by the consultant and the community agency.

The process of consultation binds the consultant and consultee in strong human relationships; and every problem solved or insight gained aids mental health in the community and prevents mental illness.

## MENTAL HEALTH EDUCATION

Mental health education involves fewer close personal relationships on a one-to-one basis than the technique of consultation. Mental health education aims to provide accurate information and encourage understanding in an effort to replace misinformation as well as to fill information gaps. Surveys seem to indicate that most people do not possess enough information about mental illness and mental health. Mental health education also seeks to help everyone gain knowledge, attitudes, and behavior patterns which will promote and sustain his or her mental health. Mental health education, ideally, is aimed at all ages and educational levels and pursues all available courses to effect action for positive mental health. Its methods range from talks, group meetings, workshops, and other gatherings to school, industry, labor, management, and civic programs; it also makes use of printed and electronic media.

Like all other prevention programs, including those for treatment, consultation and education as a community service must be responsive to needs and change and able to grow and develop with time and experience. There is great potential for helping millions of people toward mental well-being and away from mental illness through the knowledge we have acquired and by such means as those suggested.

We may not yet be able to define mental illness or mental health satisfactorily. We may never be able to. There *is* research which hints at intriguing possibilities of at least coming closer than we now are to some of the things that determine our emotional well-being. The importance for mental health of our built-in biological clocks is, for example, the subject of a fascinating scientific study. Its findings suggest that the circadian clock holds clues to the nature of mental and physical illness. The circadian rhythm or clock has to do with the twenty-four-hour measurement of a day and the light-and-darkness changes in that period. *Circa* is from the Latin, meaning "about" or "around"; *dies,* also Latin, means "day"; hence the term *circadian.* The cycle of a day is an outstanding rhythmical feature in the life of earth plants and animals. Time-lapse photography has shown that plants perform movements that follow roughly a twenty-four-hour (circadian) rhythm. All mammals are said to experience circadian rhythms of activity and rest. A study report of the National Institute of Mental Health states:

Man is no exception to this daily ebb and flow. His body temperature rises and falls in circadian tempo. His pulse and blood pressure change, as do the concentration of hormones in his blood.

In laboratory studies, almost every physiological function observed has exhibited a circadian rhythm—ranging from liver RNA, DNA, and glycogen levels, to skin mitoses, brain serotonin, and a multitude of others.*

Does our inner biological clock, setting time or rhythm for physiological functions, also influence our behavior? If so, what part does circadian rhythm play in abnormal behavior or mental illness? Investigators exploring this new frontier feel that it influences behavior and that our biological clock holds clues to the nature of mental illness. They have produced abnormal behavior and rhythms by subjecting experimental animals to behavioral stresses. With animal studies mapping the way, scientists hope to learn more about the human biological clock's functions. The report concludes:

> The role of rhythm in man's well-being has not been demonstrated, but like the suspicion that a lack of rhythmicity spells illness, animal data make one suspect that well-being in man also depends upon a knowable harmony of internal rhythms coupled with a rhythm of overall behavior, synchronized in turn with the alternation of day and night—roughly every 24 hours.

In their dramatic findings, these researchers have opened a new avenue in the understanding of mental illness. Whether or not the human biological clock turns out to be important in practical ways for controlling mental illness or making possible direct advances in mental health, this research is illustrative of the quest that is now inexorably moving us further along the road of progress toward the goal of good mental health for everyone.

*National Institute of Mental Health, *Mental Health Program Reports,* no. 2, U.S. Government Printing Office, 1968, pp. 323–351.

# MENTAL ILLNESS AT VARIOUS LIFE STAGES

## CHAPTER FIVE

Each of us lives his life in stages, which usually concur in time and thought with those of his own age peers. Medicine has been aware of this in its approaches to treating people for various ills. Many medical specialties such as pediatrics, obstetrics, gynecology, and geriatrics have developed along these lines. It is useful to look at mental illness briefly from the standpoint of its effects in the several life stages.

No attempt will be made to delve into a large number of age groupings via statistics to show how many of a specific age, sex, race, or other group are suffering from a particular kind of mental illness. Rather, a picture is sought of the problems of early, middle, and later years in broad terms. This picture will seek to show what is happening in mental illness in relation to each of the selected age categories.

## THE EARLY YEARS

Here we shall look at mental illness in the years from birth to about twenty. In the nineteenth century, mental illnesses that struck children were classified under the categories of adult mental disorders. Differentiation began toward the end of the century and picked up in the twentieth when child psychiatry became a recognized specialty and realization came that it was helpful from diagnostic and therapeutic viewpoints to focus upon the nature of mental diseases frequently occurring in children. The depth and scope of the problem of mental illness in the early years is pointed out in sobering statistics:

> As many as 500,000 children in the United States suffer from psychoses and borderline psychotic conditions.
>
> Another million children are afflicted with personality disorders.
>
> 5 million or so of the nation's 50 million school-age youngsters have moderate to severe emotional problems.
>
> 1 out of 3 of the 15 million youngsters reared in poverty has serious mental or emotional problems.
>
> 500,000 or more young people are brought into court each year for antisocial acts.
>
> Suicide is believed to be the fourth-ranking cause of death among fifteen-to-nineteen-year-olds.
>
> The number of children and adolescents in mental hospitals is increasing more rapidly than their increase in the population.

Where do all these problems of mental and emotional disorder in the young stem from? We are not sure. We do know that the foundations for mental health or illness are established in infancy and childhood. We know that major factors in adult well-being and reasonably effective and happy social adjustment are found in the physiological and psychological events of childhood.

The beginning of some of the most severe mental disorders may be traced to early childhood experiences. The origins of mental illness may lie in any stage of life. They may, indeed, be prenatal, and these we can sometimes define and diagnose. These origins of emotional or mental problems may range from unwanted conception, which could lead to poor treatment of the newborn baby, to damage to the baby's central nervous system before birth owing to viral infections or drug misuse by the expectant mother. Damage leading to mental deficiency or physical impairments which affect mental well-being can also occur during the birth process itself.

## Infancy and Childhood

Every period of infancy and childhood is of essential importance in preventing mental illness and in attaining mental health. The days, weeks, and months of the first year are certainly critical. The baby's physiological needs are entirely dependent upon the mother—or other care-giver. So, from others come the first influences that determine his personality and how he will fit into normal patterns of living.

The administration of "TLC" (tender loving care) or mothering from the earliest time of life is most important in giving the new person a good chance for mental health. Without TLC, even though his physiological needs may be fully met, his psychological development lacks an indispensable ingredient. This is true on into childhood and in fact never disappears, for who is he who never needs at least a modicum of TLC? A child avowedly does. Beginning between twelve and twenty-four months of life, the new individual leaves infancy and moves into the bewildering world of childhood.

Childhood's start, which may be said to begin with the infant's speaking rather than crying and uttering nonwords, marks the entrance of the new person into the world of communication with others. Again, TLC helps the child's mentally healthy growth, for he is molded considerably by the kind of care he receives as well as by what he hears, sees, feels, and says himself. He identifies himself, as his communication improves and his perceptions grow, with those closest to him—his mother and father or others who rear him. He identifies himself with what they do and what they are as he experiences life with them. Their relationships with each other and with others outside the family impress him enormously. These are cardinal factors in the development of his character and behavior. As the child grows, he joins extrafamilial groups, thus becoming a social being of the community and falling under influences external to his home environment.

From age three to six until age twelve through fourteen, he is sometimes gradually and sometimes abruptly brought into contact with others through preschool or kindergarten activities, school, church, and other social groups, and various media of communication such as books, newspapers, and TV. Here he finds a vast world of opportunities, challenges, frustrations, and satisfactions. He has to learn patterns of group behavior, new skills (at play or in school). He must learn to temper his aggressiveness, yet not to succumb to inert passivity. This is his first community crucible. Others confront him all his life, but he will never forget his first school days.

## Troubled Adolescence and Youth

Developments come thick and fast for a child as he makes his way into adolescence. This period of growing up is one open to mental and emotional problems; some are engendered by his physiological makeup, and others are usually bound up in the difficult business of adjusting to living with himself and others. The young person growing up often becomes very interested in a peer, usually of the same sex. They become friends, confide in each other, and spend much time together. They may join others of their age group in a discrete social cluster. Peer association may be good, if properly oriented, as through a church or school affiliation. But this kind of "good" association may not appeal to nor hold the youngsters *if it is not interesting and honest.* Associations may be "bad" if they go into violent channels, as in the case of juvenile gangs without socially acceptable goals and characterized by distinctively violent behavior.

Puberty takes the new person over the threshold from childhood into adolescence, and he experiences dramatic physiologic and psychological changes in development of the sexual organs and sexuality. The struggle to become a person, to achieve personal identity, intensifies. Independence and freedom from home and other authority may be sought in either reasonable acts or in sexuality or in aggressive, antisocial acts: crime or drug-taking, for example.

The troubled youth of today seem to some to be marching down the road of rebellion, aggression, and alienation in greater numbers and at a faster pace than ever before. But are all youth troubled like that? The majority of youth have *not* become criminals, vicious delinquents, or mentally ill. Yet it is hard to deny that shockingly large numbers of youths are manifesting a high degree of socially unacceptable behavior that is quite harmful to themselves and others. That mental illness is important here is emphasized in a fact mentioned earlier: the number of children and adolescents admitted to and resident in mental hospitals is increasing more rapidly than their increase in the population.

The proportion of youth in the population is increasing. In line with this trend, the number of youths in the population from fifteen to twenty-four is expected to increase by 36 percent or more between 1965 and 1975. But the percent of fifteen to twenty-four-year-olds in the wards of mental hospitals is predicted for the same period to *increase by 70 percent.* It may be that before many years one-half or more of the United States population will be children and youth.

Faced with these facts, social scientists as well as public and private agencies are trying to get at the basic causes of the problem of troubled youth and to provide adequate national prevention, diagnostic treatment, and rehabilitation services. Of major importance among these services specific to the mental health field is the network of comprehensive community mental health centers, which will pay particular attention to all aspects of the problems of the young.

## THE MIDDLE YEARS

If the middle ages of history were the darkest and most troubled times of all, the same may be said today for the *middle* times of the individual's life. It may not be true for the majority of those now living in *all* the years of adulthood and maturity. Nonetheless, a case can be made that the midperiod of life for millions of men and women is fraught with so much stress and trauma and ravaged so by mental illness that it may almost be termed the neglected years. It does seem to be true that the greatest attention is paid to the two end spans of life: the young and the old. They, too, have nonetheless been neglected in many ways; and they constitute the majority of the total population—so far.

But from adulthood to late maturity (ages twenty-five through sixty-five) the individual is called upon to withstand massive, continuing attacks upon his mental well-being as well as his physical good health. Both suffer. For example, cardiovascular diseases—principally heart attacks and blood vessel diseases—prematurely kill vast numbers of middle-aged people. Mental illness in all its forms ravages people in this age group; most of those suffering from schizophrenia and depression are in their middle years.

Yet these are, on the whole, the most fruitful and productive years for the greatest number of people. Men and women in this age group are perhaps too concerned with personal—or community—

endeavor and achievement to give adequate thought to their own physical and mental health. Their neglect may be unwise for others as well as for themselves because it is upon the goods and services they produce that the whole spectrum of society heavily depends. In doing themselves an injustice through oversight, they may also become unable to carry out their own chosen commitment to others. Not much, if any, attention has been focused specifically upon middle-aged people. There are pediatric and geriatric psychiatrists; and mental health centers administer children's and oldsters' service programs. The middle-aged have physicians and services available to them, but generally not in a programmatic way.

Many mental problems, as hinted, will besiege them along the way of life. There will be educational problems, marriage and its adjustments, concern about occupational successes, and social life. As the years roll on, middle adulthood brings its difficulties: job worries, financial burdens, physical sicknesses, waning sexual powers, and the heaviest load of social and financial responsibilities. The problems continue in late maturity, and to many they appear to increase. Men may look forward to retirement; women to the day the last child is grown up and leaves home. If they have not thought through and planned well for such events and for the days and years after they occur, they may be not only gravely disappointed but also badly damaged psychologically when they move into these later phases of their lives.

## THE GOLDEN YEARS

"Grow old along with me! / The best is yet to be," is the way Browning put it. In other, less euphemistic words, it can be said that it may be true, but is not necessarily so. In reference to mental illness (as in physical illness) the older years are certainly neither golden nor best. It is therefore wise to take first a deliberately dim view of the picture of old age. Having seen what the dimensions of the mental problems of the aging are, we can then proceed to discern more clearly what the prospects for fulfilling Browning's concept are. As for mental illness in the old, it bears mention that after age sixty there is a great increase in its incidence; that the great bulk of mental hospital patients is over sixty; and that the high incidence of mental and emotional disorders in oldsters is caused by both physiological and psychological factors.

Most mental disorders in old people are caused by diseases of the blood vessels (principally arteriosclerosis, or hardening of the arteries), of the brain, and of the central nervous system. These may be chronic, with gradual deterioration, or acute, with a sudden episode like a cerebral or cerebrovascular stroke. The results are seen in what is most familiarly known as senility. But it is not so well recognized that the effects of blood vessel disease of the brain, ranging from unwarranted irascibility to incoherent speech and wild, strange behavior, are not willful and are the manifestations of disease.

Modern drug therapies in particular have done much to alleviate the ravages of cardiovascular diseases and to help old people stay out of—or leave—mental hospitals, which were formerly overcrowded with older people. But there is still a long way to go before the blood-pressure-lowering drugs, anticoagulants, tranquillizers, and the other chemotherapies conquer the major physical affliction of our times, atherosclerosis (the artery-hardening disease that leads to most heart attacks and strokes), and prevent its onslaughts upon mental balance and well-being.

Another major organic cause of brain damage and consequent mental illness is senile brain disease. The symptoms of this are very much like those of the hardening of the brain arteries, in that adequate oxygen to nourish the brain is reduced or shut off from parts of the brain. In senile brain disease, the substance of the brain itself deteriorates and wastes away; the causes are still not fully known. Women are more prone than men to senile brain disease. Men, however, are stricken with cerebral atherosclerosis far more often than women, just as men have far higher incidence of coronary heart attacks. Damage done to brain cells by these organic diseases, or by physical injuries such as accidents or blows on the head, cannot be repaired. Brain cells do not regenerate; nor can they be restored. Once destroyed or decayed, they are gone forever. A great deal of research is probing into almost every conceivable aspect of the brain, however, and from some of the research frontiers, perhaps brain biochemistry, there may come new knowledge either of preventing brain-cell and tissue destruction by disease or of repairing cellular damage. Even brain-cell regeneration is not beyond promise, and some scientists feel it can be achieved.

On the side of psychological or functional causes, there are emotional disorders stemming from the development of insecurity in the aged. In the old, severe blows to the sense of security, such as the loss of a marital partner, job, home, family, or some other components of a person's familiar environment, can contribute to mental illness. Frustrations and hard circumstances can do much to bring about or intensify underlying or new functional mental disorders. Ebbing strength, sight, or hearing may do it. Loneliness and the fear of death may. Depression is common among the aged. A fearful statistic underlines this: the suicide rate among those over sixty-five is the highest of any age group.

Whether an old person's mental ailment is organically or psychologically caused is often impossible to tell, even for psychiatrists specializing in geriatrics. Whatever the causes, it is possible to help most aging patients suffering from mental illness. Good treatment and care and the application of TLC is important and will often ameliorate many of the sad symptoms of mental disorder and sometimes eliminate them, at least for a time.

Therapeutic measures which have been cited earlier in the discussion of treatment are useful for the older mental patient. Among them are good physical care, affection, appropriate physical and mental activity, recreational and occupational therapy, psychother-

apy, drugs, relief from pressures, stimulating new interests, accep-
tance of environment, and two-way understanding between the patient and those who care for him. Applied research demonstrations
have shown dramatic improvement in the aged when such measures
as these are implemented through a planned program. In one such
study, the program benefitted a majority of the aged patients in a
mental hospital who were engaged in the activity. They showed
tremendous improvement in self-care, independence, and fuller living; and many were able to return to their community or jobs.

With about 18 million older people in our population today and
25 million or so expected tomorrow—because of the partial conquest of some of the chronic diseases—the aged are certain to form
an increased proportion of the population, just as youth are at the
other end of the spectrum. Programs for maintaining, increasing,
and improving mental health in the aged, then, are already greatly
needed and are of crucial importance. The necessity and significance
of such programs are as sure to increase as is the population
of the aged.

# SPECIAL CHALLENGES
# TO MENTAL HEALTH

CHAPTER SIX

A formidable host of old and new social behavior problems challenges the individual, the community, and the health professions. Many of these social problems are as old as history, and many are as new as the subject matter of science fiction; but they all constitute part of what is known as mental illness. These problems seemingly give mental illness a more bewildering demeanor than it ever possessed before.

The names of these problems are as familiar as the news items about them in today's newspapers or television broadcasts. They lie heavily upon man's mind and in his conscience. Consider a few: Alcoholism, alienation, student rebellions, anarchism, drug abuse, racism, heedless overpopulation, crime, delinquency, violence, homosexuality, masochism, obscenity, suicide, rural deterioration, urban rot, and many other metropolitan problems.

With the unlimited problems associated with them, these may be considered members of the great family of mental illness. Or, at least they are all deterrents to mental health. If mental illness is disorganization of the individual, as has been claimed, then mental illness of society may be a greater disorganization. If this is so, then the problems cited above constitute a disorganization of the community of man.

## SOCIAL DISORGANIZATION OF A CITY

What do these problems of mental illness mean to a community? To what extent have they invaded our cities? Put together, what part do they play in the disorganization of a community?

Considering the mental health status of the community, a statement from the National Institute of Mental Health acknowledged that no average community could be found that would represent an accurate cross section of the country. A hypothetical community, therefore, was assumed, and its population given as 150,000—the size of the population to be served by a typical community mental health center. Assuming also that the hypothetical city could be found and applying national statistics, the nature of such a community's mental health disorganization was pictured:

> Three thousand children will be born in the community during the year. Among them, at least 600 will require some form of mental health service during their lifetime—240 of them in mental hospitals.
>
> In the course of a year, 225 illegitimate children are born into the community. Among those 107,000 residents above 14 years of age, over 30,000 have no more than an eighth-grade education; less than half as many have been to college.

Of the 1,200 draftees screened last year for military duty, 450—nearly 40 percent—were rejected, one third of these because they are mentally and emotionally unfit.

Each year, within the community, over 2,000 serious crimes—an average of six per day—are handled by the police, including eight murders, 17 forcible rapes, 160 assaults, 376 auto thefts, and 908 burglaries. And nearly 1,000 youngsters 10 to 17 years of age are brought before the courts annually.

The number of sleeping pills consumed is enough to supply one each night for every man, woman, and child.

During the last 12 months, nearly 150 citizens in the community attempted suicide, and 20 succeeded; in the same period, nearly 800 persons were admitted to inpatient psychiatric facilities.

There are, then, living in our average community 600 schizophrenics; tens of thousands suffering depression; nearly 4,000 alcoholics; 3,000 homosexuals; 50 narcotic addicts; and over 1,000 college students who have used marijuana or LSD; and 400 mentally ill children—nearly 100 of them in mental hospitals.

That is the profile of the mental illness disorganization of an "average American community," the statement concludes. The mental illness factors that contribute to social disorganization are many. Let us scrutinize some of the major challenges.

## SEVEN MAJOR CHALLENGES

There are common denominators among many of these serious challenges, and there are also dissimilarities. Rather than attempting to find their common denominators, here we shall discuss seven elements as individual categories. None is truly separate, but is inextricably bound to other symptoms of societal sickness—crime and narcotic addiction, for example. For our purpose, we will take a summary view of each element.

## Alcoholism

What is alcoholism? There is no universal agreement. Since the majority of informed people believe that it is a disease, they do not consider it a shameful curse or a willful wrongdoing. However, many still hold this view and feel that alcoholism is a moral rather than a medical matter.

But medical groups, including the American Medical Association and the World Health Organization, regard alcoholism as a chronic disease—a mental illness manifested in a persistent, recurring behavior disorder. The victim repeatedly drinks beverages containing alcohol. He does this so often and consumes so much alcohol that his health and social relations are damaged. The use of alcoholic beverages by the alcoholic is extreme and goes far beyond socially acceptable use.

Most definitions of alcoholism refer to a destructive dependency upon alcohol. But no precise perimeters can be drawn within which every case will fit. Diagnosis of alcoholism is largely a matter of a physician's judgment and comprehensive examination.

The American Medical Association in 1956 formally declared that "Alcoholism must be recognized as within the purview of medical practice." Other medical groups have supported this view, as have international bodies such as the World Health Organization. The courts have also begun to view alcoholism as a medical problem and to recognize that alcoholics need treatment rather than punishment.

Such a view is not generally accepted, even among physicians. Many physicians as well as those who abstain from alcohol altogether still feel that to treat alcoholism as a disease gives the alcoholic an excuse to avoid responsibility and traps him in his bottle forever.

Whatever it is, disease or sin, how much of a national problem is alcoholism? No one knows exactly. But it is assuredly vast, especially when taking into account all its degrees, from occasional excessive drinking to deep alcoholism. Alcoholism has been called the fourth greatest public health problem, outranked only by heart disease, cancer, and mental illness. In actuality, although alcoholism also figures heavily in accident statistics, it is more appropriate to regard it as a disease within the realm of mental illness.

In any event, the problem of alcoholism has wide repercussions. This is apparent when we realize that alcoholics have directly or indirectly caused hundreds of thousands of accidents, many of which result in death, severe injury, and property damage. To these must be added such consequences as the loss of job time and productivity, disruption of families, physical violence, and destruction of property. There are no accurate figures for the national burden of alcoholism. But surveys give indications of extent and trends:

77 percent of the men and 60 percent of the women of the United States drink alcoholic beverages.

Alcoholics number from 4 million to 5 million according to some estimates, which are held too low by antialcohol forces and too high by others.

Male alcoholics used to outnumber female victims 5 or 6 to 1, but some studies suggest that this has dropped to at least 4 to 1.

The risk of becoming an alcoholic if you drink at all is unknown. But this has been speculated: assuming 80 million United States drinkers and 4,500,000 alcoholics, then the risk of becoming an alcoholic if you drink would be about 5.8 percent, or 1 in 18.

Alcoholism or excessive drinking has played a role in traffic accidents and costs to industry estimated at $2 billion a year.

About 45 percent of all the 4,955,047 arrests for crime listed by the FBI for 1965 were for offenses of drunkenness—public intoxication, vagrancy, and disorderly conduct.

Dismal statistics like these are available in much greater quantity, but these suffice to illustrate the problem.When one considers what is being done about it, or should be done, the picture is even more complicated, partly because of neglect. As a government report* on alcoholism puts it: "No other national health problem has been so seriously neglected as alcoholism. Many doctors decline to accept alcoholics as patients. Most hospitals refuse to admit alcoholics. Available methods of treatment have not been widely applied. Research on alcoholism and excessive drinking has received virtually no significant support."

But there are heartening developments which promise much for the future. Social attitudes have been changing from the demand for punishment to the demand for prevention, control, and treatment. A result is that new approaches to attack alcoholism have been translated into public policy through federal legislation.

Incredible as it may seem, until 1968 no federal laws had ever been adopted to support programs for preventing and controlling alcoholism. The Volstead Act and its consequence, the Eighteenth Amendment to the Constitution, were aimed entirely at prohibiting the use of alcohol. Prohibition failed. The "Noble Experiment" of the Eighteenth Amendment was repealed in 1933, and with the exception of a few states, the nation embarked on permissive drinking. A few states continued prohibition to some degree until the mid-sixties, when Mississippi became the last state to legalize the "Demon Rum."

Oddly, for over thirty years, Congress did not legislate at all in the field of alcoholism. However, amendments enacted in 1968 to the Community Mental Health Centers Act provide for financial assistance to the development of community programs to control narcotic addiction *and alcoholism.* This marked the first time that the

*National Institute of Mental Health, *Alcohol and Alcoholism,* Government Printing Office, Washington, D.C., 1967, page iii.

need for local communities to effect programs against alcoholism had been specifically recognized by federal acts.

The National Institute of Mental Health was charged with administering the program of community support along with other major efforts to increase research, manpower, and services focused upon alcoholism. The institute's National Center for the Prevention and Control of Alcoholism was established to stimulate and support activities in all these areas. With other public and private resources, the center is engaged in a widening spectrum of activities. It provides several million dollars each year to attack alcoholism, principally through grants for research and demonstration studies.

There are two basic goals, one immediate, one long-range. The immediate goal is to make the best treatment and rehabilitation services available to all who need them. The long-range goal is to find effective, acceptable, and practical ways of preventing, treating, and controlling alcoholism.

## Behavior Rebellion

Behavior has become the monumental word of the last third of the twentieth century. Behavioral science has been coming into its own in these times, as did the "hard" sciences earlier. There is, in effect, a behavioral-science rebellion. Promising to produce no ultimate fission processes, but rather the opposite in human terms, behavioral science may bring us together before we split the world asunder.

But the times also offer what will no doubt be a delight to historians of the future: a macabre bazaar of behavior in everyday life and culture. Scientists who want to understand behavior are intensely studying its manifestations in all kinds of groups. They are probing and computing areas such as that of the hippies and other subcultures.

Seemingly bizarre behavior has always been with us and it may not be worse now than in the past. There were other epidemics: women hanging themselves in droves some 400 years before Christ; the woeful children's crusades to free the Holy Land; the burning of lepers in early France; the flagellants of this century and continent; and on and on. To chronicle these behavior epidemics adequately is far beyond the province of this book and has occupied major sociological works. But it is both interesting and important to glance at a few modern behaviorisms, particularly those which have some bearing upon increasing or decreasing mental health of the individual and the community.

There are, undoubtedly, many oddities of behavior demonstrated by what the young would consider the elderly (those from thirty to forty) and the aged (those older than forty). Their deviant or strange behavior would include alcoholism, drug abuse, and sexual experimentations such as homosexuality, mate exchanging, and, in societal terms, various perversions. Some of these are found among youth as well.

Leading to the hippies, student rebels, and racists is the process of alienation, which is so loudly proclaimed as the hallmark of the age. Alienation is regarded as one of the number of behavioral problems that include narcotics and drug abuse, school dropouts, and juvenile delinquency. Some authorities consider alienation a kind of cross-generational disease, summed up in the slogan "Don't trust anyone over thirty," said to have been devised by youth and sometimes used as a battle cry. Other critics have also referred to alienation as a "rebellion without a cause, rejection without a program, a refusal of what is without a vision of what should be."

There is nothing especially new about this. Gaps between the generations and inability to communicate across the years have been noted in every period of history, from Greek society of 2,000 years ago to the Lost Generation of the roaring twenties. It is held by authorities, however, that the crevice of alienation, in the United States at least, has been widening and separates more people than ever before.

found in national directories, listed under headings for mental illness, mental disorders, and mental health. Nearly 100 more are found in categories such as psychiatry, psychology, and related fields. Some of these are specific: American Society for Psychotherapy and Psychodrama, Academy of Psychologists in Marital Counselling, Society of Engineering Psychologists, Psychological Welfare Society. But others are broad-ranging in purpose and activities and, in effect, constitute the major mental health forces on the national level; they are private and voluntary in character. Brief sketches of some of these leading organizations will give an idea of their mission, structure, people, and activity—and of the overall nature of this phalanx of prime movers for mental health.

*American Psychiatric Association*

Numbering some 15,000 psychiatrists who have an M.D. degree (out of the nation's total of 25,000 or so), the American Psychiatric Association has a staff of skilled professionals at its national headquarters in Washington, D.C., and is affiliated with fifty or more regional groups. It is a nonprofit scientific and educational association, deriving its funds from dues, publications, and grants from government and foundations. Its objectives are to advance studies of mental disorders; to improve standards for the care and treatment of the mentally ill; to further psychiatric education; and to make psychiatric knowledge useful to other branches of medicine, to other sciences, and to public welfare. The association also assists state governments in conducting surveys of mental health resources and needs. It inspects and rates public and private mental hospitals and issues a large number and variety of publications, including books, monographs, statistical materials, and periodicals such as the *American Journal of Psychiatry* and *Psychiatric News.*

*American Psychological Association*

The American Psychological Association is a professional and scientific organization whose purpose is to advance psychology as a science, a profession, and a means of promoting human welfare. It also is headquartered in Washington, D.C., and it has a staff of 90 or more, affiliations with 52 state groups, and over 25,000 members. The association publishes a number of journals and other materials, deriving its funds from these, members' dues, and grants and awards. About 50 percent of its membership has been estimated to be clinical psychologists, who are most directly concerned with mental illness, and about one-half of this group are connected with educational institutions. The remainder are engaged in research or service in nonacademic settings. Formerly, the principal contributions of the psychologist to mental illness were considered to be in research. But this picture is not static. Certainly psychology's role has been burgeoning in education and in its participation in services and activities for the application of knowledge to benefit present or potential victims of mental illness.

## American Orthopsychiatric Association

With headquarters in New York City, the American Orthopsychiatric Association, has a small, full-time staff and draws its membership of 3,000 or more from psychiatry, psychology, social work, anthropology, sociology, education, and allied professions. Thus widespread in kinds of members, the association is also broad in purpose: "To unite and provide a common meeting ground for those engaged in the study and treatment of problems of human behavior. To foster research and spread information concerning scientific work in the field of human behavior, including all forms of abnormal behavior." It publishes periodical and other material and derives its revenues from these as well as from dues, grants, and awards.

## Other Professional Societies

Among other professional societies deeply concerned with mental health are such agencies as the Academy of Religion and Mental Health, American Association on Mental Deficiency, American Association of Psychiatric Social Workers, National League of Nursing, American Nurses' Association, National Association of Social Workers, and National Social Welfare Assembly. All these have national headquarters, annual meetings, various publications, and substantial memberships—with nursing and social work leading in numbers. They are also found at regional, state, and local levels; and their memberships are key forces in the attack on mental illness.

### National Association for Mental Health

The National Association for Mental Health is the major voluntary organization in the attack on mental illness. Founded in 1909, it has over 800 local chapters and state-level divisions, and its national headquarters is in New York City. The association is a citizens' organization which devotes itself exclusively to the total fight against mental illness and to the advancement of mental health. It sponsors research, particularly in the field of schizophrenia, selected for emphasis because of its major importance. It promotes education and training, publishes a number of periodicals and other publications, and receives its funds from grants and awards, public contributions, and publications.

It sponsors National Mental Health Week and other educational endeavors to spotlight the mental illness problem. The association helped to establish the first mental health clinic programs in the United States and has since helped to establish and staff hundreds of clinics. It affords the principal avenue for volunteer service.

### National Committee Against Mental Illness

The National Committee Against Mental Illness is an educational group of citizens and psychiatrists whose aim is to encourage and promote research, training, resources, and services aimed specifically at the prevention, treatment, and rehabilitation of mental illness. It includes many prominent individuals from public life, industry, and commerce and plays a significant stimulatory role in the field.

## National Association of State Mental Health Program Directors

Organized in 1963, the National Association of State Mental Health Program Directors is composed of state officials in charge of the specialized mental health or mental hospital programs of their states. It has a category of associate members who are directors of special community-level services for the mentally ill or mentally retarded. Its aim is to promote cooperation and the exchange of ideas and information in the administration of public mental health programs, including hospital and community care concerned with the mentally ill and with prevention.

## Other Related Organizations

There are a number of organizations which have important purposes related to mental health, but which are specialized. By way of illustration, the National Association of Coordinators of State Programs for the Mentally Retarded is a group, organized in 1963, of state administrative personnel working with programs in the field of mental retardation.

## PUBLIC AGENCIES

Most of the money, personnel, and facilities directed against mental illness in the United States come from public, tax-supported organizations. These are either general in nature, having concerns related to mental illness, or categorically created and aligned against the national problem of mental illness.

## General Governmental Agencies

On the federal level, general governmental agencies include almost every part of the executive branch, many committees and commissions set up by the President or government departments (Committee on Obscenity and Pornography, White House Conference on Children and Youth), Congressional committees, and at times, the judiciary, when court cases concern narcotics and drugs, alcoholism, and other matters related to mental illness.

Because it is unnecessary and, in practical terms, impossible to list all the mental illness involvements of all the branches of national government, it will suffice to cite several agencies. These agencies, which have considerable commitments to mental health matters such as narcotics, family planning, ghetto problems, violence, and crime and delinquency, include the Departments of Justice, Housing and Urban Development, Commerce, Agriculture, State, and Defense. (The Department of Health, Education, and Welfare, obviously, is deeply involved, but it is omitted here because it will be discussed later as the major federal endeavor specifically concerned with mental health.)

At the state and local levels, many agencies whose primary mission is not mental health are devoting time and attention on an increasing basis to its manifold challenges.

## Mental Health Governmental Agencies

The federal agency most concerned with mental health / mental illness is the Department of Health, Education, and Welfare (HEW). All components of this vast department have much to do with the national attack. Welfare is involved in such matters as birth control, social security, Medicare and Medicaid assistance to mental (as well as other) patients. Education is involved from elementary through postgraduate university programs. Although its funds and personnel are not directed toward attacking mental illness, they are inextricably interwoven into school and college mental health education.

Departmental programs that have major significance for mental health include HEW's Administration on Aging, Social Rehabilitation service (with responsibility for vocational rehabilitation and for mental-retardation services), Committee on Alcoholism, Children's Bureau, and the President's Committee on Mental Retardation. These are all concerned with development of services of various kinds and, to lesser extent and varying degrees, with research, training, and educational activities.

### National Institute of Mental Health

The purpose of the National Institute of Mental Health is, in the words of the Mental Health Act of 1946, "to improve the mental health of the people of the United States."

Placed in the health programs of the HEW, the institute is the federal government's representative in the nationwide attack on mental illness. It is the only federal agency whose entire mission is mental health. To achieve the goal set for it by Congress, the institute supports grants and conducts—through its staff or by contracts with others—the development of knowledge, manpower, and services to treat and rehabilitate the mentally ill, to prevent mental illness, and to promote and sustain mental health.

Although research is conducted in the institute's own laboratories, the major portion of research is supported by grants (which number several thousand annually) to universities and other institutions. These grants, by law and regulation, can be awarded only after recommendation by scientific and national advisory groups. Training programs for the development of manpower in mental health fields provide support to individuals through grants to institutions and through research fellowships. The development of community mental health services, including the program for comprehensive mental health centers, is aided by financial and technical assistance to the states and their communities.

The institute's programmatic organization provides for balance of effort and attention among the triumvirate of research, training, and services. It also is structured to provide special focus upon major challenges such as alcoholism, suicide, narcotic and drug abuse, and metropolitan mental health problems. The institute has some 6,500 employees located at headquarters in Chevy Chase, Maryland, just outside Washington, D.C., and in its research centers, hospitals, and HEW regional offices throughout the country. The National Institute of Mental Health was created and is sustained by public and professional interest expressed through the Mental Health Act of 1946 and continuingly through annual congressional appropriations, most of which are expended in grants and contracts throughout the United States.

### State and Local Government Mental Health Agencies

The role of state and community official agencies in the nationwide attack on mental illness represents the major, front-line assault. Since the year 1773, the states of the union have assumed responsibility for the care of the mentally ill who require hospitalization.

In numbers of people cared for, in dollars, in personnel to perform the necessary tasks, and in resources and facilities devoted to mental illness, these state and local agencies require more money, people, and facilities than everything else in the nationwide attack. Mental illness is a major financial burden upon the states; for many states it is the largest item in the budget.

There is a great deal of variation in the way states and communities have organized their mental health programs. This organization of official agencies includes the state mental health authority, mental health programs in other state agencies, state institutions for the mentally retarded, outpatient psychiatric clinics and services, and community mental health centers.

The diversion of authority and obligation among all these official agencies has caused and continues to cause problems. But there has been a trend toward coordination and uniformity, as is reflected in community mental health centers, which also illustrate the growing trend among the states to set up and develop independent mental health official authorities.

The trend toward development of mental health official agencies directed toward mental health, either in "umbrella" agencies or as independent agencies, began in the states in 1947 and has never to date been reversed. Between 1950 and 1969, there were thirty-three changes in state-level mental health administrative responsibilities. By 1969 only eight states and four territories operated their mental health programs under public health department administration. The rest, forty-two states, had given the responsibility to mental health direction rather than leaving it to the general execution of public health.

State and local governments provide support for programs in schools and for special problem areas like alcoholism, suicide prevention, and alcoholism prevention and control. Also, most of the 2,000 psychiatric clinics in the United States are supported by the official mental health agencies. Research, in community services particularly, training of manpower, and public information-education are among activities rounding out the kind of programs that public agencies throughout the land engage in.

The inventory of organizations associated with the national attack on mental illness is impressive in breadth and depth of facilities, personnel, and aims. The mobilizing, strengthening, and expanding of America's resources for mental health, which began in the 1950s, has resulted in a greatly accelerated attack through research. It has also resulted in the broadened application of knowledge by a panorama of national, state, and local organizations. The national commitment to mental health on the part of almost every kind of organization in our society establishes the point that mental health /mental illness is central to the core of our civilization and to our interest in living.

# THE BURDEN

## CHAPTER NINE

Mental illness strikes more frequently, attacks more people, requires more prolonged treatment, causes more suffering by the individual and by his family and friends, wastes more human resources, takes up more buildings and other facilities, and consumes more of the personal finances of the individual and his family and the public taxes than any other disease.

This is true in the United States and in many other countries. It is believed by some that primitive or underdeveloped peoples had less mental illness because they were not burdened with the pressures of civilization. This has not been proved by epidemiological studies.

*Epidemiology* is a term, largely appropriated by medical science but also used elsewhere, meaning the study of the spread and causes of diseases. The Greek root word *epidemia* means "among the people." Today, epidemiology is a chief investigative tool of medicine and, more than that, a scientific profession. Epidemiology in a sense is detective work; it traces and analyzes the how, when, where, why, what, and among whom of diseases. This study is not limited to epidemics or sudden, wide outbreaks of illness; but it also deals with incidence (rate at which a disease strikes), prevalence (how much of it there is at a given time in a given population), and mortality. Epidemiology seeks to delineate the characteristics of a disease and the significant facts related to it. For example, an epidemiological study concerning schizophrenia will involve gathering and analyzing data on the number of patients in mental hospitals as well as other facts, such as the duration of their stay and how they came to be there.

Such measurements, then, are the essence of epidemiology and furnish indispensable information which may be useful in giving clues concerning the prevention or control of a disease. Epidemiological studies uncovered the fact that some babies were born with defective brains because their mothers had contracted German measles during pregnancy.

Statistics on disease are also essential in planning for services and facilities to take care of afflicted people. Epidemiological studies of what happened to the populations of mental hospitals over a period of years following introduction of the tranquilizing drugs have been invaluable. They played an important part in some of the foundation work resulting in the development of the community mental health centers program that ended complete reliance on the old custodial mental health hospital.

## MEASUREMENT OF MORBIDITY

Morbidity has to do with the statistics of the state of unhealthiness or disease. Epidemiology in the field of mental illness, with respect to morbidity, has been more difficult than in other, easier-to-diagnose diseases. It is comparable to the state of an underdeveloped country contrasted with an industrialized one. Epidemiology has made many contributions, but it is only in very recent years that its horizons have expanded. Thus, morbidity facts on mental illness are far from being as comprehensive as one might wish. Yet they do give us at least an impressionistic picture of the occurrence and amount of mental illness.

## Numbers of People Afflicted

Mental illness has no equal in terms of social destructiveness of the individual, his family, and the community. In sheer numbers, its prevalence is tremendous. About 1 in every 10 persons in the United States is now suffering from some form of mental illness. It has been estimated that about 19 million people are afflicted. This figure has been fairly constant over a number of years, and opinion seems to be that mental illness is not increasing—at least not rapidly. One reason is that it is not illegal for physicians or others to refrain from reporting a case of mental illness. Since usually there is no infectiousness or contagion associated with mental disorders, it has never been a spreading public-health menace like smallpox. Thus, physicians are not required to report cases of mental illness, as they are of many infectious diseases, and available figures are not as reliable as they are for infectious diseases.

Nevertheless, interesting and indicative figures on mental illness are obtained and recorded. In 1844, a report showed that there were an estimated 17,400 "insane and idiotic" persons in the United States. In a total population of around 17 million, this meant that about 1 out of 977 people were mentally ill.

England, Belgium, Holland, and France were said to have similar ratios; their proportion of mentally ill ran from 1 in 846 (England) to 1 in 1,014 (Belgium). The incidence in Spain (1 in 7,180) and Italy (1 in 4,876) was higher, for unexplained reasons. Much of this was based upon data from mental hospitals, or "lunatic asylums" as they were called in 1844 (and up to a few years ago). Much of today's statistical information comes from studies in connection with mental and other hospitals where the bulk of patients still go, although there is a growing trend away from the long-term stay in a mental hospital.

A study showing where mental patients received treatment in 1965 indicates that 1,657,000 persons went to hospitals. These were state, county, or private mental hospitals; general hospitals; and veterans' hospitals. The remainder of the 3,921,000 mental patients estimated to have received treatment in 1965 obtained it through outpatient clinics, psychiatric day-night units, and private-office care. The National Committee Against Mental Illness and the National Institute of Mental Health have compiled illuminating facts about incidence, prevalence, and mortality associated with mental illness. Among the more striking facts are these:

> Mental illness or other personality disturbances are involved in criminal behavior, delinquency, suicide, alcoholism, and narcotics addiction.
>
> Suicide is the tenth leading cause of death in the United States.
>
> Suicide, by conservative estimates, causes 25,000 or more deaths each year.
>
> Drug addicts number at least 100,000 persons in the United States.

At least 50 percent of the millions of medical and surgical cases treated by private doctors and hospitals have a mental illness complication. Emotional disturbances and mental illness are an important factor in the cause of 75 percent of all accidents.

Other studies show continuing high amounts and effects of mental illness. It has been a major affliction among the U.S. Armed Forces and a main cause of Selective Service rejection. This is as true

today as it was during World War II, when 4.8 million draft rejec-
tions—18 percent, or 1 in every 5—was for mental illness. Of the 1
million disability discharges from the Armed Forces during World
War II, 43 percent were for neuropsychiatric reasons—with the
next leading cause at 12 percent. The residual of this is in part
reflected in the 140,000 veterans who were receiving mental illness
treatment in 1965 in Veterans' Administration hospitals.

## MEASUREMENT OF SOCIAL AND HUMAN COSTS

There are few measurements of the social and human costs of
mental illness. These are subjective values and to say that 1 million
homes were disrupted by mental or emotional disorders brings
little compassionate understanding. The cost to society and to the
individual and his family in nondollar terms *can* be understood by
examining what physicians call the case history.

This book is not the place for *full* presentations of this kind. Many
copious works are readily available in most public libraries. Often
their whole content is case-history material on mental illnesses.
These can help provide an in-depth background for understanding
the devastating toll exacted of every mentally ill human being and
his associates. Visits to mental institutions or clinics can provide an
even deeper understanding.

Here we illustrate the point by brief glimpses into two case histories. The presentation of all details is unnecessary, since all we
have to see is their effects at a particular time. The first case is
realistic, though hypothetical.

> John Needham was an accountant in a leading department store
> when, in the fall of 1948, he began to suffer extreme anxiety and
> tension. His family doctor prescribed some pills and told him to
> take it easy. Although the medicine helped for a time, it was
> impossible for Needham to slow down.

His family and coworkers became more and more concerned as
the months went by, but they were helpless. The community was
a sizable one and had a psychiatrist. But the prevailing sentiment
in Needham's circle was not favorable to consulting the doctor.

"Nobody goes to a psychiatrist unless he's crazy," they said.

One night a terrified Mrs. Needham called the family doctor.
Her husband was holding a conversation with an imaginary person. The doctor, after seeing Needham, arranged for an emer-
gency court hearing. Needham was committed to the state hospital, 150 miles away, with a diagnosis of schizophrenia. There was
no local general hospital nor other facility near his home that
accepted psychiatric patients. Ten years later, in 1958, John
Needham was still in the state mental hospital.

Now and then, but more and more rarely, he saw his wife and
children, and almost never a friend. The meetings were always
painful for all of them. In the mid-50s, the hospital, like others,
began using the tranquilizing drugs. But Needham was one of
those patients whom the drugs helped very little if at all.

And so we turn from John Needham, who may still be found in the
state hospital, to another, younger "case" from the same source
and, again, without a real name.

In the fading days of the summer of 1965, in our nation's capital,
there is living an eleven-year-old boy. Call him Billy Jones, call
him alive, but not much more. He spends his nights huddled in
apartment hallways. He is not alone. He has the only friend he
knows—a stray dog as homeless as himself.

While thousands of his young fellow citizens begin their return
to school, he skulks in alleys, deserted buildings, and the eu-
phemistically named "low-income dwellings" of the slums and
ghetto. Somehow he ekes out food for himself and his friend dog
from apartment tenants. Then one day he is "found," spotted by
police as a waif, and taken to a detention home. He is also found
now, through years of neglect, to be mentally retarded.

Billy's story unfolds. His meager decade of life began in a broken home. He ricocheted from court to welfare department, from mother to foster home, from institution to psychiatrist. He had been tested, but never treated. He had been examined, but never loved. So it was that he had begun to spend his own love on dogs, not people, and to try to live with a dog rather than with humans.

Cases such as these measure the social and human costs and burden of mental illness.

## MEASUREMENT OF ECONOMIC COSTS

The dollar cost of mental illness in the United States is estimated to be almost $20 billion a year. When this is known, it is difficult to be more emphatic or dramatic about the economic burden of mental illness carried by every individual. The sick person is bereft (as are the rest of us) both of the fun of living and of funds. He usually goes broke, and we pay for his care. The matter is not one to take lightly. Not humor nor lightness nor stoicism can serve useful purpose here.

But it is helpful to look calmly at some of the components of this $20 billion cost. These can be broken down into the costs of

Reduction of productive activity among the mentally ill

Treating the mentally ill

Illegal and other undesirable behavior attributable to the effects of mental illness

Intangible psychic loss that so often accompanies mental illness

These components all fit into the picture when the cost of mental illness is defined as the loss of well-being suffered by society as a result of this disease. A summary of the categories of costs fills in the big picture titled: "$20 billion."

## Reduction of Productive Activity

Reduction of productive activity has three parts which, in aggregate, make up the largest category of material costs of mental illness:

1   Loss of marketable output: it is estimated that mental illness reduced this output by $14.3 billion in 1966.

2   Loss of homemaking services: the cost of loss of services in homes of mentally ill women totally unable to carry on this activity because of their illness is estimated at being $970 million in 1966.

3   Loss of unpaid work: this means work done around the house such as painting and yard maintenance, charitable voluntary work, and recreational activities. Called speculative, but probably conservative, the estimate for the year's period is $250 million.

## Treatment and Prevention Cost

Treatment and prevention is the second major category of cost and is estimated *in toto* to have amounted to almost $4 billion in 1966. Some components of this big bill are:

1   Inpatient-care cost: over $2.5 billion.

2   Outpatient-care facilities: over $1 billion.

3   Development of mental health facilities: $121 million.

4   Training mental health personnel: $94 million.

5   Research in mental illness: $113 million.

6   Management expense of operating government agencies concerned with mental health: although no estimates are available on the costs of managing state and local mental health official agencies, the management cost of the National Institute of Mental Health in 1966 was put at almost $20 million.

## Illegal and Other Undesirable Behavior Cost

Thefts, assaults, homicides, and other crimes are often attributed to mental illness, as are accidents and behavior stemming from mental illness that leads to avoidable divorces, disharmonious family relationships, excessive gambling, promiscuity, illegitimacy, alcoholism, drug addiction, and so on. Firm estimates have not been made on dollar costs of these effects of mental illness.

One example of these costs, however, is the estimate that many narcotics addicts steal or otherwise illegally obtain (as by prostitution) $30,000 each year in money or goods to secure their addictive drugs. Other examples, without dollar figures, include the estimates that alcoholism contributes to over 50 percent of all fatal automobile accidents and to over 20 percent of all industrial accidents.

*Intangible Costs*

As was mentioned earlier, intangible costs are impossible to measure in the terms used for most of the other groupings. It can be brought home again, though, by taking another look at the case of John Needham.

We left Needham in the mental hospital, where he still is. We saw or sensed the intangibles of insecurity, bewilderment, frustration, hopelessness, bitterness, loss of self-esteem, fear, anxiety. Not included in this bill of particulars is the tangible bill of costs. The costs of Needham's case lie in the $4 billion per year spent nationally for treatment and care. The total bill for John Needham for the first ten years of his mental hospital stay added up to about $11,000—paid for by taxpayers.

His own funds ran out early; and his family managed (rather poorly) by his wife's working, which she was able to do because their children were old enough to be left alone. This did save taxpayers the cost of welfare payments to her. But, on the basis of Needham's average earnings prior to hospitalization, his illness for the first ten years meant a loss of about $50,000 to his family and society.

Billy Jones, our other "case history," had no family to worry about nor any job to lose. Nor will most of the Billy Jones's ever have. They will, like him, eventually be found in an institution.

There, then, are John Needham and Billy Jones, privileged and underprivileged, two casualties representing not unusual costs nor extraordinary cases in the mental illness war.

It has been estimated that the per capita yearly cost for mental illness in the United States is about $48. The estimates we have are far from perfect, but we know the burden is enormous. There is also an enormous need for more funds for many aspects of the national attack on mental illness.

What may be equally or even more needed is the warm, positive, informed interest of every individual in doing something about mental illness—and, most important, more people going into mental health work. The mental health forces are critically in need of manpower. The costs of mental illness will never be reduced as substantially as is now possible unless there are more mental health recruits.

# MANPOWER: NEEDS & OPPORTUNITIES

## CHAPTER TEN

The major studies of the early sixties, conducted by the Joint Commission on Mental Illness and Health, called the matter of professional manpower a dilemma, and since that period, the situation has continued to be marked by crying needs and whispering opportunities. The dilemma is that there will never be enough professional people available to care for mental patients (in the face of an increasing population) without commensurate increases in the recruitment and training of mental health workers.

Every other health field faces the same difficulty. Manpower shortages are acute in the ranks of all the health professions. The shortage of physicians in general has been most publicized. New medical schools have been established, and existing schools have expanded their programs. The number of physicians has been increasing, but not fast enough. It is doubtful whether there will ever be enough physicians to provide an adequate amount and a high quality of medical care for all demands.

By comparison with other health fields, the mental health field has not done badly in recruiting the training manpower. In fact, it has outstripped all the others. Between 1960 and 1965, the growth in major general health professions (medicine, dentistry, environmental health, nursing, and health research) was 18 percent. In the same period, the growth in the major mental disciplines (psychiatry, psychology, psychiatric social work, psychiatric nursing), was 44 percent.

The mental health professions have, indeed, shown a steady and encouraging increase since 1950. In 1950, there were engaged in mental health work 10,000 nurses, 2,000 psychiatric social workers, 3,000 psychologists, 10,000 psychiatrists—a total of 25,000. By 1967, this had grown to a force of 22,000 nurses, 13,000 social workers, 15,000 psychologists, and 20,000 psychiatrists—a total of 70,000.

Not only the increase in population, but also the remarkable growth in the kinds of essential mental health services has accounted for these gains in manpower. It has also caused professional personnel in the mental health field to divide their working hours among a number of facilities.

## CRYING NEEDS

Some sense of the crying need for more mental health manpower has already been gained from the statistical picture of the burden. That there are 700,000 to 800,000 patients in mental hospitals while nearly 4 million are being treated for mental illness underline these needs.

Surveys have shown that patients in state mental hospitals do not receive adequate care and that modern treatment therapies cannot be provided owing to a severe lack of personnel. The ratio of physicians to patients in state mental hospitals was found to be about 1 to 100 patients. This ratio may be compared to the American Psychiatric Association's minimum standards for care which require that there be 1 physician to each 30 patients in admission and intensive-treatment services and additional physicians for other services such as continued treatment and geriatric care.

Critically inadequate ratios of professional and service personnel also exist in state as well as other mental hospitals. These include shortages of clinical psychologists, psychiatric social workers, registered nurses, occupational and recreational therapists, and many others such as attendants, maintenance employees, kitchen workers, medical-record personnel, teachers, and business-office employees.

Fully representative statistics are not available to indicate how many workers are needed to serve in the mental health forces with the physician, psychologist, social worker, and nurse. However, it is obvious that there are thousands of jobs open for these kinds of workers in hospitals alone. Unfilled positions in professional job categories further indicate stark needs, according to various compilations of manpower data by the National Institute of Mental Health:

> About 1 in every 4 budgeted positions for staff psychiatrists is unfilled in Veterans Administration hospitals and state hospitals for the mentally ill and mentally retarded.
>
> 21 state mental hospitals were found without even 1 psychiatrist.
>
> 91 state mental hospitals were found to have only from 1 to 4 psychiatrists
>
> 7 positions were offered for every 3 clinical psychologists applying in 1963, the American Psychological Association Placement Office reported.
>
> 1 out of every 4 budgeted positions for registered nurses in state

mental hospitals and institutions for the mentally retarded was unfilled in 1963; and the situation has hardly improved since.

Most of the needs are in the mental hospitals. It is far more difficult to obtain from clinics and community centers, by questionnaires or any other means, sound statistics about the kinds of jobs that exist, how many are filled, how many more are needed, and so on.

Again, however, it is inescapable that many positions go unfilled because a huge personnel is needed to provide services in the more than 2,000 clinics and community mental health centers in the United States. There is unanimous agreement that many more people are needed to work against mental illness and for mental health.

Deciding which kinds of personnel are most needed and how many workers in other areas should be recruited and trained, however, does not elicit agreement. The competition for training funds is great, particularly among proponents of the needs for the core disciplines of psychiatry, psychology, social work, and nursing.

Yet, it must be pointed out that these professions are also encouraging the development of other kinds of mental health workers and are engaged in teaching and training people of widely divergent occupations. In the four core disciplines themselves, the current manpower pool is estimated to be 75,000, with a modest but difficult goal of 100,000 for 1972. No one thinks that this will be in excess of the need.

Rather, projections indicate that the mental health manpower shortage will continue unless the rate of output of professional personnel increases. This has not occurred in the years since the commission's gloomy portrayal of the manpower dilemma. For anyone with a spark of interest for work in the field it is an area of widening and challenging opportunity.

## WHISPERING OPPORTUNITIES

The opportunities for the whole spectrum of mental health workers have not been publicized as much as the needs. A National Institute of Mental Health report says: "No segment or level of the mental health manpower pool can be considered to be adequately supplied at present; to attempt to assign priorities to given elements of the pool and ignore others would only create further imbalance and problems. Alleviation of shortages must occur 'across the board.'" A look at career opportunities across the board is now in order.

*Nursing*

There are well over 600,000 active professional nurses in the United States, making nursing the largest health profession. All nurses, by the nature of their profession, engage in mental health work. But the number involved in full-time work in the mental health establishments (about 22,000) is a small percentage of the whole group.

Although the number of mental health nurses has been growing, there is a need for even more; and the opportunities today and tomorrow are far-ranging and stimulating. Mental hospitals, of course, are a prime area for a variety of nursing opportunities. The increasing number of psychiatric services and wards in general hospitals are in need of more psychiatric nurses.

Changing approaches to the problem of mental illness have moved the attack into the community and greatly expanded the opportunities for mental health nurses. The work of nurses has dramatically shifted from purely custodial care to dynamic participation in prevention, treatment, and rehabilitation programs.

Community mental health centers are responsible in great part for this increase in opportunities and are likely to generate more.

Nurses engaged in mental health fields have a variety of educational backgrounds. A survey reveals that nurses in some 2,000 mental health institutions and facilities ranged thus in education: 3.6 percent with graduate degrees, 9.3 percent with some graduate training, 11.4 percent with bachelor's degrees, and 74.8 percent with three-year diplomas or less than three years of training.

Are there many opportunities for would-be nurses and for those already in nursing to obtain training and develop a career in mental health? The answer is a resounding Yes! As much as or more than any profession, this field is wide open to both young and old today. Not only training but also jobs are available throughout the United States. And, it should be emphasized, the profession is one which men may enter; they are encouraged to undertake it, and they can find satisfying and challenging jobs. As in teaching, there are not enough men. Men can fulfill a unique function in direct nursing care of mental patients as models for these patients, who must learn to respond to and cooperate with persons of both sexes.

Men can also engage in administrative jobs in nursing services, in teaching positions in nursing colleges and other educational institutions, in industrial consultant positions, and in community mental health center programs. None of this is to underplay the need for young women—and mature and even senior women—to engage in mental health work from foster care of babies to rehabilitative services for oldsters in mental hospitals or nursing homes.

The cardinal point is that there are opportunities for both sexes and for all ages. Perhaps what is needed in part is a concept similar to that of the Peace Corps or VISTA. It would not seem outrageous if, in view of the problem and the need for people to cope with it, there were a brave new program of service for mental health, under which people would be recruited, trained, and supported with reasonable salaries.

Returning to present prospects, we can easily see that there is a great demand for mental health nurses in other areas. Industry and labor are affording new opportunities. The Armed Forces have need for nurses trained in psychiatry. Public and private agencies in the community, such as schools and health and welfare agencies, are looking for nurses who can provide mental health consultation and services.

Many avenues are open to those who want to embark upon a career in mental health nursing. To mention only two, there are technical nurse training and professional nurse training. If a person does not or cannot attend college for four years, there are two alternatives, both technical training courses: the Associate Degree and the hospital diploma programs.

Graduates of these technical courses are eligible to take state examinations for registered nurses. These and other jobs that will place one in a psychiatric setting are available to those taking technical training. The Associate Degree program is usually a two-year program offered by a community or junior college. The hospital diploma program is offered by a hospital training school and runs from two and one-half to three years. It may also include academic courses in a neighboring college.

Professional nurse training involves getting a four-year college degree, a B.A., B.S., or B.S.N. (Bachelor of Science in Nursing), a professional course in which the student attends regular college classes and studies clinical nursing in hospitals and other health agencies. With the bachelor's degree, the nursing graduate can take a state examination to obtain a registered nurse certificate (license to practice). He or she can then seek specialty training (as in psychiatry) or work toward a master's or higher degree. A career that can be rewarding though demanding may immediately be entered upon.

Anyone can start planning a mental health career in high school. For example, the school nurse or health department or local mental health association will—or should—be glad to help an interested person begin. When launching a nursing career, one should explore fully all the possibilities for financial assistance for training if assistance is needed. There ia a great variety of assistance programs, from undergraduate aid to postgraduate (from predoctoral through doctoral) fellowships available today from individual colleges and universities, foundations, various associations, and public and private mental health agencies.

## Psychiatry

To become a psychiatrist (which means to obtain a degree as a doctor of medicine as well as specialized training in psychiatry) requires at least eight years of medical and specialist education beyond the four-year bachelor's degree in college.

No doubt this rigorous training acts as a deterrent, but the fact is that there have been increasing numbers of individuals who have sought and entered into this demanding career. From society's standpoint, it is discouraging that most of these doctors have gone into the private practice of psychiatry. This restricts their utility to the community since they see and help far less of the mentally ill than do those psychiatrists who practice community psychiatry and engage in public service full-time.

The rewards of private practice, with an average earned by the psychiatrist in the United States of about $49,000 per year, are probably not the only reason. Another reason might be that neither the medical schools, the general medical professions, the communities, nor other concerned agencies have done enough to encourage community psychiatry. Another reason might be that community psychiatry is, after all, very young. It will take more time to integrate community mental health therapies deeply enough into psychiatry to change the whole pattern.

While it is the most demanding mental health profession in requirements, psychiatry offers the greatest challenges, with the possible exception of psychology. Moreover, psychiatry offers not only great opportunities for service to many people, but also the greatest opportunities to enter full- or part-time research. It is also a major avenue into teaching and training and to a large number of high-level posts such as directors and administrators of many kinds of institutions and programs on the local, state, or national level.

Undertaking a career as a psychiatrist is an endeavor that requires intellectual exercise and hard work, but it is not a mission only for the elite. Psychiatrists are not gods or demons or comic figures, contemporary portrayals to the contrary.

Many more young people *could* enter the profession than are doing so. Perhaps too many are frightened off by the wrong images of the psychiatrist, the long and expensive course to become one, or the feeling that they are either not worthy or not capable. Many are, therefore, not seriously considering psychiatry as a career. They may not obtain adequate information upon which to base a sound judgment. They may be relying on scanty information—or misinformation.

But there are good sources of information on psychiatry, and they are, generally, as helpful as possible so that one can establish a reasonable basis for decision. Psychiatry has not been as attractive a career as it might be because it has not been publicized as a field where important discoveries are made, where one can help people in a real and demonstrable way, and where there are real social, intellectual, and financial returns.

No doubt many youngsters considered cardiovascular surgery as a career after the first human heart transplant and the continuing marvels of natural and mechanical spare-parts operations. Psychiatry has not made such spectacular advances, but it has helped more people to useful lives and well-being than has any surgical procedure.

Psychiatry and the other mental health professions are making important discoveries, helping people in very real ways, and rewarding their workers rather satisfactorily. The demand for psychiatrists is rising more rapidly than the present output can expect to supply. The program of community mental health centers and the Medicare program will place more and more demands upon the profession.

With the burgeoning problems of the cities—racial discrimination, crime and violence, and students and schools—it is apparent that special-area psychiatry programs will have to expand in such fields as community action, mental retardation, crime and delinquency, pediatrics, and geriatrics.

Generally, these are some of the opportunities in psychiatry. An inquiry into the field will quickly show that it is full of solid, brains-and-action kinds of work as specific as helping suicidal patients, an abandoned retarded child, or a roomful of despairing drug addicts.

*Psychology*

There are also many opportunities in the field of psychology. In a sense, it is a profession of even vaster scope than psychiatry, since its sphere of activity is not confined to mental health matters. Those jobs that are directly involved in mental health are of concern here. They are, to put it mildly, opportunities of quite a wide range. A marked growth has taken pace since World War II in the entire field of psychology. Within this frame, there has also been a considerable increase in numbers and interests of psychologists in mental health.

The primary organization in the field, the American Psychological Association, has been growing. The association had 18,215 members in 1960. In 1965 it consisted of 23,561 members. With respect to mental health work on the part of the nation's psychologists, a 1964 National Science Foundation Register survey of psychologists found that 69 percent of 16,800 psychologists responding to the survey felt that their work was relevant to mental health.

What do psychologists do for mental health? Of all mental health professions, they are the most active in research. Nearly one-fourth of those in the 1964 National Science Foundation study said that research was their most important job activity. But the greatest numbers of psychologists are engaged in the mental health field in psychotherapy, in diagnostic as well as other kinds of testing, and in teaching.

As in other work concerned with mental illness, the work of the psychologist is expanding in new directions, particularly in connection with programs and concepts of the new community mental health centers. Thus, there are more opportunities in both research and service aspects of psychology today than ever before.

Psychology has attracted many young people because it is a field useful to them in other careers. However, for the vast and increasing needs of the mental health field, the supply of psychologists has not yet met the demands, and it does not appear that any saturation point will be reached for a long time.

There are, and likely always will be, many fascinating and satisfying opportunities for psychologists in mental health work. These opportunities are at various levels and of many kinds from technical positions to research directors. Those with the college degree, the master's, postgraduate work, or the doctoral degree in psychology may find that mental health work has much to offer.

## Social Work

Next to nursing, social work contributes the largest number of professional personnel to the mental health field. In 1960 it was estimated that there were about 116,000 social-welfare personnel in the United States, and by 1965 this was estimated to have grown to not less than 125,000. The number has continued to increase.

In nursing as in other fields, it is difficult to estimate what number of these people is engaged in mental health work or what percentage of their time is devoted to it. The psychiatric social worker obviously is completely committed to mental health. But his colleague, the social worker in a welfare agency, may be almost wholly occupied with the emotional problems of his clients, and thus be an almost equal member of the mental health team.

The range of kinds of social work in mental health is extremely wide, as are the educational requirements for the positions involved. Social workers are found in a variety of public and private agencies serving the public; they are essential to all health and welfare agencies such as hospitals, clinics, and service centers. In many agencies, social workers serve as the first therapeutic point of contact for the clients—the mentally ill and their families. They also work with other agencies, from corporations to courts, in behalf of their patients. But social work is by no means confined to service activities alone. Teaching and training as well as research are major endeavors in social work.

Education for social work ranges from the doctoral, master's and bachelor's degrees to associate degrees and special training courses with or without academic credits. High school graduates are engaged in social work of certain kinds; and more and more agencies are providing career-development training and on-the-job opportunities for those of various educational backgrounds.

The challenge and the diversity of opportunity for people who want to serve their fellow men are suggested by the fact that social work is carried out by people with particular knowledges, competences, and values which are designed to help individuals, groups, or communities toward a mutual adjustment.

*Beyond the "Core" Disciplines*

Psychiatry, psychology, nursing, and social work are the four disciplines central to the attack on mental illness and the march toward mental health. As we have noted, many other indispensable skills are directed toward the establishment of mental health. There are severe shortages of these skills in most instances. Moreover, so many new occupations and jobs are developing (that do not require doctoral or even college degrees) that it is difficult to catalog them.

Some of the more common and innovative of these occupations suggest the nature of the new frontiers in mental health. They reveal strikingly that mental health work is "for real," that it is where the action is, that it deals with relevant issues, and that it has to get out of the cloistered halls of clinics and go where the people are.

But these occupations also show that mental clinics and hospitals must have more and better health workers to turn snake pits and dumping grounds into places of healing. The need for psychiatric aides is an example.

*Psychiatric Aides*

There are estimated to be 100,000 or more psychiatric aides and attendants in psychiatric hospitals—not enough to provide the services needed. There are, however, other aspects to the problem. Turnover among psychiatric aides is 25 percent per year or more. Salaries are too low; many aides earn less than minimally adequate annual living wages, although the picture is changing. Also, training opportunities to improve and increase skills are not uncommon, nor are career development opportunities.

Many factors contribute to the manpower problem from both the patient's and the aide's viewpoint. There are too few aides for the number of patients; the aides lack training to give adequate skilled help, though many have lifted themselves by their bootstraps, as it were; and the facilities and surroundings are too often not only inadequate, but also retrogressive rather than progressive in nature. In recent years, efforts have been increasing to improve these conditions: to raise salaries, to provide training, and to make the work more rewarding.

There is a long way to go, but a start has been made to improve this important occupation. Some demonstration projects, supported by government or private funds, have shown that programs involving the training of aides and others can be successful—if there are competent staffs, therapeutic surroundings, and various activities for the mental patients.

## Occupational Therapists

Although numerically a relatively small field, with about 8,000 occupational therapists in 1967 engaged in mental health work, occupational therapy is an important and growing one. Standards, requirements, and the kinds of jobs and job training are all changing, as is the case, of course, in other health fields.

Generally, the trends seem to be toward specializing in a single treatment area, for example, in the rehabilitation of mental patients in a state mental hospital. Occupational therapy in this area, as in most other mental health areas, would be concerned more with psychological than physical rehabilitation. That is, the therapist in a field other than that of mental illness usually is mainly concerned with a patient's mastering physical skills, such as learning to walk with an artificial leg after loss of a limb or developing writing ability with the left hand after a stroke.

In the mental hospital, the therapist is occupied with getting the patient to socialize and to readjust to community living and work situations satisfactorily. These kinds of things are as important—or more so—as the actual job skill the mental patient is taught. Training for the occupational therapist deals with both psychological and physical measures, however, and covers a four-year college program. Physical and biological sciences, psychology, sociology, and some humanities and arts-and-crafts courses generally are comprised by the program. A Bachelor of Science degree in occupational therapy is obtained, and some months of supervised practice follow.

It almost goes without saying that occupational therapists are in great demand. One has only to think of the tremendous needs in all health fields for skilled people who can aid rehabilitation. By comparison with the great and growing demand, the production of occupational therapists from the colleges is a small trickle that will never fill the need.

The mental health field hopes to improve its position to some degree at least—and it will, if it can increase both the support of training of occupational therapists and the quality of job opportunities. Some prospects for this are seen in the community mental health centers and mental hospitals' improvement programs.

## The Clergy and Police

In earliest times, the clergy were first and foremost among those who dealt with mental illness. Priesthood and medicine went hand in hand. They still do, but in quite different ways. There has been at times in recent history as much separation of church and medicine as there has been of church and state. The separation between the clergyman and the psychiatrist in the past century may or may not have been too wide. Whether this is true or not, some evidence indicates that they are more closely associated today.

This is sensible, for people as well as for these vocations. After all, next to general physicians, the clergy see more people with emotional difficulties than do any professional workers, in part because there are 330,000 or more clergymen in the United States and less than 250,000 physicians.

In addition to the general practitioners, policemen and clergy are the only ones to whom many people bring their emotional problems. Clergymen and policemen, then, have come to be recognized as important members of the mental health service forces. Activities for the training of clergymen in mental health have been underway for some years and are increasing. More recently, the role of the policeman and the need for training him have been coming to the fore; and there are encouraging educational programs for all levels of policemen that aid them to better deal with and understand the bewildering problems of mental and emotional disorders.

*New Kinds of Mental Health Workers*

While efforts have been directed toward increasing the manpower of the core disciplines and related professional personnel, efforts have also been launched to train new kinds of workers for mental health programs.

A good deal of attention is being paid to the training and utilization of people who carry out under professional supervision a variety of duties which used to be performed only by professionals with academic degrees, special training, and experience. Exploratory programs have indicated that it is becoming increasingly feasible to use people in mental health work who have high school, junior college, or college-level educations and who are given some mental health training and supervision by fully trained professionals.

Major efforts in this direction have been made by government and private agencies in the mental health field and with the cooperative participation of junior colleges, colleges, and universities. These efforts include the relatively new idea of employing indigenous workers in mental health programs, particularly in urban areas. The idea of using nonprofessionals to supplement professional personnel in social agencies is not new. What is new in this mental health endeavor is the systematic, in-depth approach to the finding, training, and using of people—with or without educational qualifications—who live in the neighborhood where work is needed.

The community mental health aide, as he is sometimes called, can considerably supplement and complement the professional's work. Although he may be limited in education, he knows the people, the setting, and the day-to-day problems. And he lives among the people with whom he is to be in contact.

Other efforts in creating new kinds of mental health workers include programs to train mature housewives as rehabilitation workers, volunteers (both men and women) to provide new and effective services in hospitals and for community mental health centers, and disadvantaged youth to enter the health service professions.

Programs are also being carried on to train mental health workers at the Associate of Arts degree level. These are some of the continuing experimentations to turn out new kinds of mental health personnel. They range from short-term basic training, nonacademic in character to longer courses of a few months, one to four years in college, and postgraduate work of a wide variety.

In sum, there are many critical needs as well as dramatic opportunities in mental health manpower. Salaries and working conditions can be either good or poor. Training programs can be innovative as well as traditional. Because of the ferment and the endless variety of tasks to be performed, the challenges of mental health as a career are uniquely appealing.

# GAINS & FUTURES

## CHAPTER ELEVEN

Where are we in the war against mental illness and in the progress toward mental health? Are we gaining or losing?

Use of the word *war* when speaking of mental illness implies an aggression that is anathema not only to advocates of mental health, but also to less optimistic colleagues, particularly clinical psychiatrists, who work daily against mental illness and have minimal hope of reaching the ideal of mental health for everyone. Even if we abandon the familiar simile of war and adopt less dramatic terms, there are difficulties.

To determine where we stand we must know where we were at some point in the past. But we have never really known enough about the nature and extent of mental illness. In discussing the current state of affairs, there is no solid foundation which one can compare. Nor are there adequate indicators today. Yet a general sense of the state of mental health, and indications of progress in some areas and deterioration in others, can be obtained.

Each age has felt that it was on the most terrifying brink of disaster ever known. Each of us marches along sharper edges of deeper chasms than did our forerunners. Our times are more frightening, debilitating, and conducive to mental and emotional degeneration than any in man's history. We are right to feel so. No others' experience can be as acute, meaningful, penetrating, and close to home as our own—and unless we feel that a thing is bad and getting worse, we may be disinclined to do something about it.

This is true in the mental health/mental illness revolution; and we are stirred to many efforts to reduce mental illness and advance mental health. We do this even though there is no overwhelming evidence to indicate that mental illness is more prevalent, strikes more heavily and rapidly, or is more virulent today than it was formerly. Nor, on the other hand, can we definitely conclude that the problems of mental illness are less pressing. Summarizing prevalence and trends in mental health and illness, "Toward A Social Report" (published by the U.S. Department of Health, Education, and Welfare in 1969) states:

> It is difficult to know with certainty whether mental illness represents an area of improvement or a growing problem. Because of unsolved problems of psychiatric diagnosis, and because the types of behavior that are considered manifestations of mental illness change with our culture, no adequate measures of the mental health of a population have been developed. There is, accordingly, very little nationwide data on the prevalence of emotional disturbance in the population.
>
> Local surveys have been carried out in the United States to determine the prevalence of mental disorders, but their results do not lend themselves to comparison. Despite the lack of comparability

among studies, each shows that sizeable proportions of the population studied suffer or have suffered from a mental disorder.

Data on trends in mental health status are also limited. Only for the most serious and incapacitating forms of mental illness which require hospital care do the data allow any judgments about changes over time.

The data suggest that there is a continuing and significant annual reduction in resident mental-hospital populations, and therefore, that progress is being made toward mental health, even though this progress is difficult. At least we can be sure that more people are being better treated for mental illness, that there are useful ways and means both of therapy and of prevention, and that there is developing an attitude that mental illness is not willful, shameful, or hopeless.

Along with this, there is the optimistic observation that we are not losing ground previously won, that we are proceeding into new territories of therapy, and that we can and must find the causes of and solutions to the many new and special challenges to mental health. Some may disagree with this rosy picture, but it profits little to adopt a negative rather than a positive approach to the mental health situation that confronts us as we move into the twenty-first century. We prefer the optimistic to the pessimistic view because

1   We can show there are still 700,000 persons in mental hospitals; we can be sure that there will be thousands in hospitals for years to come. And yet we can show that substantial reductions, long hoped for, in mental hospital populations have been made, are increasing, and will bring the number down to about 176,000 by the time the United States is 200 years old in 1976.

2   We can show that, darkly, there are incurable vast numbers of schizophrenics and unreached numbers of sufferers from depression who will seek suicide as their cure. And yet we can show that schizophrenia is being successfully treated (more cases could be if brought to care earlier), and possibilities exist for revolutionary

breakthroughs in the drug treatment of depression and of schizophrenia.

Is the total endeavor for mental health a mammoth revolution in progress or merely a sputtering rebellion? Or is the effort either a *rebellion* or a *revolution?* These terms imply the overthrow of existing states. In the sense of breaking away from the customary, established shackles of mental illness the effort is a rebellion hoping to become a revolution. In the sense that it is a search for better ways of life, the endeavor is not at all the kind of conflict that the analogies of rebellion and revolution imply. Rather, it is a quest for well-being by Homo sapiens, as an individual and in groups, through methods such as research, education, and the application of knowledge to make more of mankind healthier. These are proud generalizations. What are the specific advances upon which such statements stand?

## GAINS OF THESE TIMES

Since many recent gains against mental illness have been described in previous chapters, only a brief highlighting of major accomplishments is given here. Less than a score of years ago, psychiatry had no clearly useful drug treatment for schizophrenia or other mental illnesses. Research has given the physician powerful weapons in drug compounds of a wide variety. Collaborative hospital research studies helped define the relative value of specific drugs.

Drugs have shortened the patient's hospital stay and made treatment and rehabilitation in the community possible for increasing numbers of the mentally ill. Meanwhile, there has been progress in biological research. Laboratory studies of brain biochemistry have provided groundwork for clinical studies, such as those designed to perfect promising drug treatment of depression. On another basic front, the role of biological rhythms in psychological and physiological health is the subject of focused research by burgeoning numbers of investigators; important new knowledge is accruing and one day will be of great usefulness.

Behavioral-science studies have provided such a broad spectrum of step-by-step research findings that it is impossible to capsule their knowledge gains. The accretion of information in three broad fields exemplifies, however, these kinds of advances: better understanding of attitude and personality development, uncovering origins of aggressive behavior, and turning computers to use in inquiries into the basis of man's intellectual functions.

Research aimed at gathering information to help solve specific, major mental health problems has produced results. For example, new effects of barbiturate use have been discovered; the real, factual patterns of alcohol use in the United States were brought out by careful survey studies; and useful data were provided describing personal characteristics associated with suicide.

Further examples of research findings show the range and depth of scientific gains:

> A compound found in the urine of schizophrenic patients bears a close chemical resemblance to drugs which evoke psychotic experiences in normal people.
>
> An abnormal protein factor isolated in the blood of schizophrenics has been used to differentiate accurately between twins, one of them schizophrenic and the other normal.
>
> Information that suggests discernible differences in brain-wave patterns between psychotics and normal individuals has been obtained through computer developments, making possible a more detailed exploration of the electrical activity of the brain.
>
> Although biological and biochemical research in schizophrenia continues to indicate that some forms of the disease arise from an abnormality in the body's biochemical and neurological functions, painstaking studies of the relative incidence of schizophre-

nia in twin populations make it seem that hereditary factors also play an important part in the disease's origins.

The development of conditioned learning techniques in psychological laboratories has made the teaching machine a valuable tool for retraining schizophrenics, rehabilitating brain-injury patients, and raising the intellectual level of the retarded.

Such creative research must coincide with the production of skilled manpower, the provision of new and improved facilities, and the development of effective service programs. Recent gains in these three areas have been impressive.

First, as was mentioned in the preceding chapter, considerable gains have been made in the numbers and kinds of manpower in the mental health field; manpower has grown at a considerably greater rate than it has for other health professions. There are still far from enough workers of all kinds engaged in mental health, but the numbers are still apparently increasing. Mental health training has been bold and vigorous. Many advances have been made in the education and training, from undergraduate through post graduate levels, of the four core disciplines in professional mental health work.

But there have also been stimulating and encouraging developments in new fields. New kinds of mental health workers have come into being, ranging from aides with high school or less to junior-college graduates and on to post-graduate workers. People of all occupations have been given mental health training and enlisted as full- or part-time members of mental health teams.

The provision of new and improved facilities to treat and care for the mentally ill—and to prevent mental illness and promote mental health—is another gain of our times. It has occurred mainly along two major fronts: in hospitals and in nonhospital, community-integrated buildings.

Far from all public or private state, county, and local mental hospitals have made the advances they should have made and would like to make; nor have all non-mental hospitals which have or could have psychiatric wards or beds for mental patients. But there have been major and minor improvements. Many hospitals are no longer merely dumping grounds—way stations to the grave.

The hospital-improvement program (established in 1964) of the National Institute of Mental Health has been responsible for federal support in this field. With hospital associations, psychiatric and medical societies, and others joining in the enterprise, significant gains have been made in the improvement of mental hospitals in the United States. For example, the program has provided financial support through grants for hospitals in every state to undertake improvement projects they could not otherwise have carried out. The results have been impressive.

Improvements in therapeutic services reached over a quarter of a million hospital patients in five years. Over 60,000 hospital staff members were helped to translate existing knowledge into more effective service. Yet there is still vast room for improvement in mental hospitals, as staff of the institutions are first to proclaim.

In today's contexts of alienation, protest, and new behaviors, the patients and staff of mental hospitals may be more alienated than most, might protest more rightfully, and could shock with their behavior more strongly if they chose. So far, they have not. They have displayed greater sensitivity, restraint, and rationality to the outside world than it has to them. Still, gains have been made in the hospitals and, even more encouragingly, in the almost spectacular development of community facilities.

The country's growing network of community mental health centers is the focus of this major advance. The centers' aim is to provide new and dynamic community facilities and the manpower to staff them. Their goal is to make available a wide range of community-based diagnostic, treatment, aftercare, and rehabilitation resources to everyone. The centers, in various stages of development, are found in congested core cities, sprawling suburbs, and sparsely populated rural areas. All segments of the population are to be served: young and old, farmer and factory worker, welfare recipient and fee-for-service patient.

The geographic and demographic breadth of the program for community mental health centers is paralleled by the increasing kind and number of public and private organizations that participate in their development and growth. More than 1,000 organizations have taken part in the program and contributed time, talents, and other resources into the centers' careful planning and sound local administration. In addition to public and private mental health agencies, these organizations include universities, social service agencies, clinics, educational groups, and civic clubs. This dramatic cooperative enterprise of public and private interests is in itself a dynamic and important step forward and makes health care possible in what has too long been a neglected area.

Just as there have been gains in research, manpower, and facilities, there have been considerable service achievements. These have been detailed especially in terms of the advances in the prevention, treatment, and rehabilitation of mental illness. The gains in treatment, for example, manifest in modern therapies of many kinds have made the last twenty years among the most remarkable in man's history for progress in dealing with mental disorders. Rehabilitation has made many gains as well, and it is at the core of many hospital, clinic, and community programs today. We see its evidences in the growing numbers of mentally restored who have returned to their homes and jobs. Prevention has not fared as well, but it has not been without gains, and research suggests that it will have future days of greatness.

The public image of the mentally ill has improved, although the shame-and-shun reaction of people to mental disorders is still far too prevalent. Public awareness of some of the facts about mental illness and mental health has increased a great deal. People seem to need and want greater knowledge about mental health matters. They also want to be provided with more mental health/mental illness information than even those most deeply involved in the problem ordinarily realize.

Much of this kind of information which the public is eager to have is not, of course, recognized by them as related to mental matters. An example is information about narcotic and drug abuse: they are related to emotional disorders, yet they are not usually associated with sickness unless one stops to consider the problem in depth.

From an overall view, the major areas of research, training, services, and application of knowledge are expected to progress; the rate of growth and improvement depends upon such things as break-throughs, which would speed up affairs, or large increases in funds, which would expedite both the spread of knowledge and its benefits.

Considered as national efforts toward mental health, advances in areas already explored have been predicted for the next few years:

> The widening and deepening of research to uncover knowledge about mental illness and mental health
>
> Redoubling of efforts to increase and maintain in adequate numbers the kinds of mental health workers needed in all areas
>
> Establishment of nearly 500 community mental health centers with bold architectural innovations in their facilities by the end of 1970; raising this number to 1,500 by 1980 and to 2,000 by the year 2000 or earlier
>
> Expansion of public and private health insurance to provide better protection for more people
>
> Improvement and expansion of such mental health services for children and youth as health examinations, counseling, and treatment

Continuing development of major efforts to provide the disadvantaged with mental health information, treatment, care, and rehabilitation

Provision of alcoholism, drug-addiction, and delinquency facilities and treatment services in cooperation with community mental health centers and other resources throughout the country

Development on a vast (and now improbable) scale of family-planning and population-control services to dampen the population explosion

Continuing efforts to improve state laws related to the treatment of the mentally ill

Similar efforts to improve the nation's mental hospitals and make them places of care and effective treatment rather than dumping grounds

Protection and promotion of mental health as well as prevention and reduction of mental illness through improved housing, strengthened education, better welfare aid, and job training, and other environmental-health programs

Depending upon one's point of view, these eleven programmatic predictions may seem sanguine or conservative; adequate or insufficient; or probable, possible, impossible. Any or all of the eleven may be thrown out of balance or demolished if, for example, some tremendous discovery is made.

Suppose a real cure for the many manifestations of schizophrenia should be discovered? Already there are hints, even beliefs, that this not only is possible, but also is on the way. Genetic and hereditary clues are piling up. A molecular theory of origin and treatment, involving biochemical means, has been urged. Millions of dollars, much modern technology, many facilities, and considerable scientific brainpower are focusing upon schizophrenia.

It has been said early in this book that finding the key to schizophrenia will be comparable to the conquest of syphilis. Though not yet complete, work toward this conquest began in 1944, when it was discovered that penicillin could cure early syphilis. Prior to that time it had supposedly been proved that the antibiotic was useless against syphilis, but it turned out to be an effective cure of the early form of the disease.

Throughout history, man had sought a cure for syphilis. It was not until early in the twentieth century that one was found: Paul Ehrlich's "magic bullets"—arsenic compounds. But treatment was difficult and required over a year to complete. The 1944 discovery was important because it eradicated syphilis with a few shots of penicillin. Later only one shot became necessary. Moreover, penicillin was a prophylactive (preventive) measure. Improved hygiene, widening public knowledge about venereal disease, expanded programs of case finding and treatment services, and the universal availability of an inexpensive, effective cure brought syphilis to defeat.

To be sure, the disease is still a problem, and it will be for as long as people do not take advantage of current knowledge, either because they are disadvantaged or for other reasons. But syphilis is no longer a killer and crippler—filling hospitals with the dying.

This kind of success could happen in the field of schizophrenia. But we cannot tell when, how, or by whom the cure will be discovered. If we cannot be sure of these things, we can pretty safely venture that other problems needing our attention will arise. This has been true in medical history and involves, among other things, the nature of man and his environment, and what he does to both. As a disease or condition has yielded to advancing knowledge, new aspects of it have developed, or other underlying health problems have been revealed and have grown. This may well go on until man becomes the perfectly healthy being, in body and mind, that he dreams of.

That day is not yet here, and it may never arrive; but this does not mean that the health progress being made is useless. We are slowly, perhaps imperceptibly, becoming at least a little healthier physically all the time—and it cannot be proved that man is deteriorating mentally.

In any case, it is certain that we shall have mental health problems in the future, whatever advances are made. Consider the fact that in a few years *one-half* the population of the United States will be young people, most of them *under age twenty-five*. At the other end of the scale will be the aged—people *over age sixty*, who will constitute *one-third* or more of the population.

Thus, the young and the old will constitute 80 to 90 percent of the population, and the middle-aged (those between ages twenty-five and sixty), about 10 to 20 percent. Since the middle-aged produce the most and pay most of the taxes, they will have to increase their gross product considerably if things continue as they are, and they must provide the major share of support for the other 80 to 90 percent as well as for themselves.

Whatever happens, we can be sure that the shifting age of the population is going to pose mental health problems. And there are many other present (and certainly increasing) problems that ensure the jobs of those engaged in mental health work. Urban crowding, overpopulation, racism, pollution of air and water, rampant technology, genetic modeling, mind control by drugs, warfare, and civil violence are a few.

In the face of all this, where will we be tomorrow? It is proposed that we must commit ourselves to the thesis that progress for good is possible and that, however slowly, human society is progressing.

In this context, a component of progress is the growth of mental health and the diminution of mental illness. That these will be achieved in presently unforeseeable dimensions is not an irrational speculation, nor is a general and optimistic conclusion that by the year 2000 the average person will likely possess far better mental well-being than he does today.

# ADDITIONAL READING

ACKERKNECHT, E. H.: *A Short History of Medicine*, The Ronald Press Company, New York, 1955.

ALEXANDER, F. G., and S. T. SELESNICK: *The History of Psychiatry*, Harper & Row, Publishers, Incorporated, New York, 1966.

ARNHOFF, F. N., E. RUBINSTEIN, and J. C. SPEISMAN (eds): *Manpower for Mental Health*, Aldine Publishing Company, Chicago, 1969.

BAADE, F.: *The Race to the Year 2000* (translated from the German by Ernst Pavel), Doubleday & Company, Inc., New York, 1962.

BERNE, E.: *A Layman's Guide to Psychiatry and Psychoanalysis*, Simon and Schuster, Inc., New York, 1968.

CASTIGLIONI, A.: *A History of Medicine*, Alfred A. Knopf, Inc., New York, 1947.

DEUTSCH, A., and H. FISHMAN (eds.): *The Encyclopedia of Mental Health* (6 vols.), Franklin Watts, Inc., New York, 1963.

———: *The Mentally Ill in America*, Columbia University Press, New York, 1962.

COHEN, S.: *The Drug Dilemma*, McGraw-Hill Book Company, New York, 1969.

ERON, L. D. (ed.): *The Classification of Behavioral Diseases*, Aldine Publishing Company, Chicago, 1966.

EYSENCK, H. J.: *Fact and Fiction in Psychology*, Penguin Books Inc.—Pelican Book no. A696, Longmans Canada Ltd., Don Mills, Ontario, Canada, 1965.

GINOTT, H. G.: *Group Psychotherapy with Children*, McGraw-Hill Book Company, New York, 1961.

GRAHAM, H. D. and T. R. GURR, (eds.): *The History of Violence in America*, report to the National Commission on the Causes and Prevention of Violence, Frederick A. Praeger Inc. and Bantam Books, Inc. New York, 1969.

GRAHAM, T. F.: *Stars and Shadows: Mental Health in Ancient Times*, Beacon-Bell Books, Canton, Ohio, 1967.

HALPERT, H. P.: *Public Opinions and Attitudes about Mental Illness*, U.S. Government Printing Office, Washington, 1963.

HOGBEN, L.: *Science for the Citizen*, George Allen and Unwin, Ltd., London, 1956.

HOWELLS, J. G.: *Family Psychiatry*, Charles C Thomas, Publisher, Springfield, Illinois, 1963.

JACKSON, D. D. (ed.): *The Etiology of Schizophrenia*, Basic Books, Inc., Publishers, New York, 1960.

JAHODA, M.: *Current Concepts of Positive Mental Health*, Joint Commission on Mental Illness and Health Monograph Series no. 1, Basic Books, Inc., Publishers, New York, 1958.

JOINT COMMISSION ON MENTAL ILLNESS AND MENTAL HEALTH, *Action For Mental Health*, final report to the U.S. Congress, submitted to the Congress, Dec. 31, 1960, Science Editions, John Wiley and Sons, Inc., Basic Books, Inc., Publishers, New York, 1961.

KATZ, M., J. O. COLE, and W. E. BARTON (eds): *The Role and Methodology of Classification in Psychiatry and Psychopathology*, U.S. Government Printing Office, Washington, 1968.

McKOWN, R.: *Pioneers in Mental Health*, Dodd, Mead & Company, Inc., New York, 1961.

MENNINGER, K.: *The Vital Balance: The Vital Process in Mental Health and Mental Illness*, Viking Press, Inc., New York, 1964.

MERSHEY, H. and W. L. TONGE: *Psychiatric Illness, Diagnosis and Management for General Practitioners and Students*, The Williams & Wilkins Company, Baltimore, 1965.

NATIONAL COMMISSION ON MENTAL HEALTH MANPOWER: *Careers in Psychiatry*, The Macmillan Company, New York, 1968.

NOYES, A. P., and L. C. KOLB: *Modern Clinical Psychiatry*, W. B. Saunders Company, Philadelphia, 1966.

NUNNALLY, J. C., JR.: *Popular Conceptions of Mental Health*, Holt, Rinehart and Winston, Inc., New York, 1961.

RICHTER, D., et al. (eds.): *Aspects of Psychiatric Research*, Oxford University Press, London, 1962.

RIDENOUR, N.: *Mental Health Education*, Mental Health Materials Center, New York, 1969.

———.: *Mental Health in the United States*, Harvard University Press, Cambridge, Mass., 1961.

RINKEL, M. (ed.): *Biological Treatment of Mental Illness*, L. C. Page & Company, Farrar, Strauss & Giroux, New York, 1966.

SELLS, S. B. (ed.): *The Definition and Measurement of Mental Health*, U.S. Government Printing Office, Washington, 1968.

SINGER, C., and E. A. UNDERWOOD: *A Short History of Medicine*, Oxford University Press, New York, 1962.

SODDY, K., and R. AHRENFELDT, (eds.): *Mental Health in the Ser-*

*vice of the Community*, J. B. Lippincott Company, Philadelphia, 1967.

SWERLING, I., *Alienation and the Mental Health Professions*, Vir-
ginia Commonwealth University, Richmond, 1968.

USDIN, E., and D. H. EFRON (eds.): *Psychotropic Drugs and Related Compounds*, U.S. Government Printing Office,
Washington, D.C., 1967.

WILLIAMS, R. H., and L. OZARIN (eds.): *Community Mental
Health—an International Perspective*, Jossey-Bass, Inc.,
San Francisco, 1968.

169

# INDEX